PLANTS ARE MY FAVORITE PEOPLE

Alessia Resta

WITH VIVAN LEE

PLANTS

MY FAVO

PEOP

ILLUSTRATIONS BY LUCILA PERINI

ARE
RITE
LE

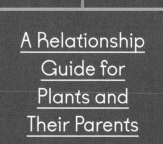

A Relationship
Guide for
Plants and
Their Parents

CLARKSON POTTER/PUBLISHERS

NEW YORK

Library of Congress Cataloging-in-Publication Data
Names: Resta, Alessia, author.
Title: Plants are my favorite people : a relationship guide for plants and
    their parents / Alessia Resta.
Description: New York : Clarkson Potter, [2022] | Includes index.
Identifiers: LCCN 2021008436 (print) | LCCN 2021008437 (ebook) | ISBN
    9780593233771 (hardcover) | ISBN 9780593233788 (ebook)
Subjects: LCSH: Indoor gardening.
Classification: LCC SB419 .R447 2022 (print) | LCC SB419 (ebook) | DDC
    635.9/65--dc23
LC record available at https://lccn.loc.gov/2021008436
LC ebook record available at https://lccn.loc.gov/2021008437

ISBN 978-0-593-23377-1
Ebook ISBN 978-0-593-23378-8

Printed in China

Book design by Danielle Deschenes

10 9 8 7 6 5 4 3 2 1

First Edition

For old and new plant lovers
who keep the world growing

CONTENTS

HOW PLANTS BECAME MY FAVORITE PEOPLE

I'm Alessia Resta, artist, gamer, plant mom, and creator of the Instagram @apartmentbotanist.

As a child, I always knew I would be an artist. When I finally had the chance to study art, I went to college at the School of Visual Arts in New York City, where my main concentration was sculpture and bio-art. I fell in love with the physical forms we find in nature—in particular, plants and sea life. During my studies, I started to wonder how these plants and sea creatures would behave if they could use social media. In doing my thesis work, I started buying plants for how they looked without really considering the fundamental needs they required to survive. I was creating terrariums and experimenting with different ways to design installations with plants and turn them, along with other nature-inspired imagery, into sculptures. But I was also killing plants—a ton of plants. I was a total plant-care novice, and it took years of asking questions (the same ones I receive on my Instagram) to learn everything I now share with my followers and am about to share with you.

After I graduated, I was running my own business, dealing with some health issues, and beginning to show my work in galleries. With life moving at a fast pace, I really craved a release. I started looking for hobbies and outlets that I could use to calm my anxieties and cultivate positivity. I saw the growing plant collection in my tiny apartment and realized that what had been a passive distraction in my hectic life had started to become something much more meaningful.

I began researching the scientific names of my plants and where they were native to so I could understand the environment in which they would thrive. I realized that some of the cacti I owned would never flourish unless I was willing to actively control the environment by altering the light and temperature to suit their needs. At the same time, I didn't quite have the time or temperament to commit to all that. I definitely wasn't *yet* the type of plant parent I wanted to be. I was still learning how to balance my time and career, all while trying to find a sturdy place for my feet to land.

Years later, I was spending a lot of my time cooped up in my New York City apartment. In February 2017, I thought it would be ironic, challenging, and funny to attempt to be my own botanical garden and keep rare plants in this city apartment. I also liked the idea that visiting my apartment might give someone the chance to see and experience a plant they might never have the opportunity to see otherwise. My little idea finally sprouted and grew into my Instagram account, *Apartment Botanist.*

I created the account in hopes that its lightheartedness would bring similar happiness to my followers and give folks a taste of what it's like caring for an indoor jungle in a concrete one. Now I care for over 200 plants—a nice mix of rare and common houseplants—in my 750-square-foot apartment on New York's Upper West Side. With *Apartment Botanist*, I began turning all the things I learned (and wished I had learned earlier) into tips and tricks for plant novices to help them have fun and experiment with plants. I love that I can be the difference that helps people gain that much-needed "plant confidence."

On top of it all, caring for my plants also helped me care for myself. I began developing a natural bond with my foliage friends. If I neglected my needs, my plants would also get overlooked. Seeing them like that pushed me to pull myself together and take better care of myself so that I could care for my plants, my boyfriend, Micah, and my two canine assistants, Pachino and Zeus, to the best of my ability.

I love housing and caring for all these plants. Despite the lack of space in our apartment, we've made it work and have tied that into our decor. Our plants are part of our unique little family, and we love it that way. Caring for plants has also helped me in so many unexpected ways. Plants not only have taught me about patience and taking my time but also have improved my general well-being and brought so much positivity into my life. I've also made lifelong friends by sharing my plant failures and successes on my Instagram account and in real life; I meet up with them to go plant shopping (more on this on page 163) and even trade propagated plants (learn more on page 161). *Apartment Botanist* has helped me foster a large local and international community of plant lovers, allowing me to connect with millions of plant parents online and create a plant-care (and self-care) support system.

Nurturing my collection, becoming involved in this community, and maintaining *Apartment Botanist* helped me realize how far I've come since I started on my plant journey and all the remarkable and unexpected positive things plants have introduced into my life—they even brought me here, writing this book for you. Everyone will have a different experience with plants, but opening yourself up to happiness and the lessons they will teach you are the first steps on your journey.

This book is a culmination of my many years of knowledge gained from buying, collecting, and caring for plants. Whether you just want a few plants to spruce up a sunny spot or crave a floor-to-ceiling collection that rivals a rainforest, this is the guide for you. We'll figure out your plant-parent personality (take the quiz on page 31), which plants will work for you and your space (including those unexpected choices!), and the ins and outs of plant shopping (and avoiding plant scammers). Just as not all plants are alike, not all plant advice applies across the board. I hope to guide you on your plant journey so you can understand what you and your environment have to offer.

Plants have subtle characteristics that make them unique, but when it comes down to it, plants are my favorite people because they *always* are worth the work. I have gained as much from them as I have put into them. Building that relationship with my plants has been the most rewarding part of my plant-parent journey, and I hope to help you on your journey to discovering the magic of plants.

HOW TO USE THIS BOOK

This book is written with the intention of guiding you as you become a plant parent. It's a book meant for readers to keep revisiting as they develop their plant confidence. Along with discovering information about plants that you might pair best with, it allows you to identify the type of plant parent you might be (and how you might change as you grow into this hobby). The Plant Parent Quiz (page 31) is meant to change results as you move along your plant path.

Think of this book as a set of tools to guide you as you grow and change as a plant parent. Come back to it whenever you need a quick tip or boost in confidence, or need to learn more about your plant-parent identity (or even re-take the quiz!). This book will encourage you and give you a place to start. You're the author and the artist of your own plant-parent journey; I'm just here to show you the possibilities.

FAQ

I had so many questions when I first started. I didn't know who or where to turn for answers, so a lot of my time was spent piecing information together. Now I pass my knowledge and experience on to you. Here are some of the most common questions I receive via *Apartment Botanist*.

1. **What Is "plant confidence"?**

   Plant confidence is feeling assured in your abilities when you succeed with plants and not losing hope when a plant dies in your care. It's also about appreciating all the happy and bad mistakes that can—and will—happen, which teach you the most about your plants and the type of plant parent you are or have become.

   The thing I want most for all you plant parents out there is that you develop and strengthen your plant confidence. Plant confidence grows stronger the further along your plant journey you go. If I had quit after every plant I killed, I would have never gotten to the place I am now with my collection! Likewise, if I had let my plant successes go to my head, I would never have challenged myself to introduce new plants into my space.

2. **Do plants actually purify the air?**

   Whether or not plants act as a natural purifier is one of the biggest topics of discussion in the plant community. While many people point to their plants as improving their mood and mental health, there is no evidence to indicate that plants in general—or individual plants—purify the air. Scientists have studied this topic under controlled conditions and have found no way to prove this theory. While data has confirmed that plants can help increase the amount of oxygen in a room, that amount is only measurable in large quantities, like an entire forest ecosystem.

3. **What is the best light for my plant?**

   Finding out the type of light that is available in your space is essential to understanding what your environment has to offer. The best way to learn this is to study your space:

What does the light look like throughout the day? Do you have bright mornings and shady afternoons? Is it bright all day long? Can you see the actual sun outside your window (in other words, direct light)? Once you know how light behaves in a space, you can begin to evaluate the types of plants you can successfully add to your collection. Keep in mind that experimenting is the spice of life; you might be surprised what plants do well in your space. And if you are dealing with a very low to no-light situation, you can still get creative with grow lights, terrariums, and vivariums.

4. **Does window size matter?**

    The size of a window only matters in terms of its *abundance* of light. In other words, the window size determines how *much* light (no matter the type; think of it as an amplifier—or not) of that light. So while you may not have floor-to-ceiling windows, knowing the amount of light your window is letting in is a good thing to consider when finding the plant real estate for your home.

5. **Does it matter what plant I bring home?**

    Yes! Before bringing home the plant, you should inspect the leaves and soil and look at its overall health and appearance. Plants can have pests, and bringing an infested plant home could create a problem for you—especially if you already have a growing collection. When it comes to those pests, inspect the leaves by first checking the top and undersides for markings, like small yellow spots. Most pests will hide on the back of the leaves or in the plant's nooks and crannies, so don't forget to give the stem and soil a peek, too. If anything looks suspicious, ask for some help or pass on that plant. You should inspect the new plant closely for pests when it enters your space, but also pay attention to early signs of new growth and lush healthy leaves. Also, plants sometimes get stressed in new environments, so give them time to acclimate to their new light, temperature, and overall space.

6. **How do I acclimate my plants to indoor life?**
Assuming you properly inspected your plant before you brought it home, you should isolate that plant for two to three weeks. This isolation time is to help rule out pests, as most pest life cycles will surface in that time. That isolation could vary based on your space. At the very least, the plant(s) you're isolating should be placed several feet away from all your others, saving your babies from a disastrous pest infestation or disease. The isolation period is also a great way to allow time for the plant to get used to the temperature and light of its new home. Plants can take several weeks to months to acclimate to a new space. Factors like level of maturity (juvenile plants are more delicate) and the establishment of new roots play a big role in how long plants can take to adjust. A good sign of successful acclimation is new growth on the plant; it means that the roots are growing and the plant is satisfied in its new home!

7. **How do I treat plant bugs?**
One day, I noticed white stuff moving all through my succulent terrariums. I dove into my research and found out those cottonlike critters were mealybugs, and they devastated my entire collection.

Treating pests is never an easy task, especially when it becomes an uphill battle to save your plants. First, you need to isolate affected plants from the rest of the collection.

A year into my plant journey, I purchased a variegated banana tree, which at the time was the most expensive plant purchase I had ever made. It was over $100, and I still remember how nervous I was when I hit that "Place Order" button.

As you might have guessed, I proceeded to make many mistakes. First, I assumed that the plant would arrive mature, established, and ready to join my burgeoning collection. (Hot tip: When buying a plant sight unseen, never assume the maturity of the plant until you have it in front of you.) Then I thought that the care for this plant would be similar to other tropical plants I had, which I quickly found out was *not* the case. I had also done absolutely no research, so when I received it, I was in no way ready for what came out of the box. It looked like a stump with a bonelike piece of stem sticking out from the top that made the whole thing look like a cartoonish severed foot.

What I didn't realize at the time was that it was just the rhizome (the swollen root), which I now know is normal for this plant. It grew quickly, and I immediately realized that I was not ready for this plant. With tons of help from the online plant community, I gathered information and started growing that tragic-looking mess into a true beauty. It got massive over the course of a month and soon hit the ceiling in my apartment. It was on one sunny afternoon that some light webbing caught my eye. I discovered the plant had a spider mite infestation, which I later learned was common for banana trees. I had zero idea how to handle it, and the infestation eventually spread to my surrounding plants. I was devastated and tried all the wrong, and overly aggressive, treatments to save this plant I had worked so hard to grow—which, of course, only made it worse. I made one last-ditch effort to save it, but the whole thing ended up rotting. It was devastating to say the least, but that was a very important crash course on some plant-care basics.

I had excitedly documented the unveiling and growth of the banana tree on *Apartment Botanist*, but now I had to cut its life and fame short. I realized my favorite aspect of having that plant wasn't actually owning and growing it, but the effect it had on other people, including myself. It was an emotional roller coaster from its rhizome beginning to its tragic rotten ending.

I'VE BEEN THERE!

Once, I purchased a beautiful dieffenbachia for my parents for their outdoor space, and when the temperatures dropped, they decided to bring it inside. Well, this beautiful dieffenbachia turned out to be infested with spider mites. In order to protect the rest of their plants, I first instructed my dad to isolate the plant, then rinse and treat it. But even after all that, its health was on the decline. I had to break the news to my parents that it was time to say goodbye and try again in the spring, with some preventative treatments. Bidding a plant farewell is never easy, but sometimes it's the best thing for you and your plant collection.

Prep the surface areas by disinfecting them. Second, identify the type of pest you may have. Some of the most common ones are mealybugs and other types of scale insects, spider mites, aphids, fungus gnats, and thrips, but a quick internet search will usually tell you what you need to know. Now comes the treatment, and it may vary based on the pest and your personal preference (i.e., natural remedies versus chemical options). Most treatments involve cleaning the plant and pot band and likely changing the soil, which I highly suggest. You also want to research how often you should treat the plant, based on the pest's life cycle.

Even if you follow all these steps, you may unfortunately have to say goodbye to your plant before it infects the rest of your collection. This part is never easy, but sometimes it's the only solution.

8. **Do I have to repot my plant?**

If you can, I suggest repotting your plant when you first bring it home. It will not only help you eliminate any bug hitchhikers but also set up your plant for long-term success. Normally, plants that are ready to sell in their nursing pots also are ready to graduate to a more permanent pot. The key is to find a pot that is about 2 inches bigger (in diameter) than the nursing pot. (See "How to Repot a Plant" on page 29.)

9. **How do I water my plants?**

This is actually a more complicated question than you might think! There are so many components that go into watering your plants. For example, you have to consider the material and size of your pot, how much light your plant is getting, the soil or planting medium, the temperature and humidity of the environment, and where your plant is in its growth cycle.

But for now, start by watering your plants thoroughly at their base, where they meet the soil, and pour slowly until water comes out of the pot's drainage hole. Keeping a structured care schedule is paramount. For plants that need to be watered more often, pot them in plastic and use a moisture-retaining potting medium instead of, say, a terra-cotta pot with a looser, more aerated medium (check out the "At-Home Soil Recipes" on page 69 to learn more).

I have my plants on a weekly watering routine, but each one gets its own special treatment. I like to think of plant care in daily, weekly, and monthly terms. This helps break down small and big tasks. Don't worry; I'll dive into all the details in part III.

TRY NOT TO GET ANY WATER TRAPPED ANYWHERE IN THE BASE OF THE PLANT OR IN BETWEEN THE STEMS; IT COULD CAUSE YOUR PLANT TO ROT.

10. **Can I just mist my humidity-loving plants?**

Collecting rare plants, and even some of the more common ones, I quickly realized that my dry and temperate New York City apartment was not an ideal environment for them. Since most of us don't have the pleasure of living in a lush paradise, a mister (aka spray bottle) is a great tool to have, especially during the growing season. I personally use a mister to help unfurling leaves open, which comes in handy for my philodendrons. If you don't have a humidifier in your home, a mister is a great solution.

What you should be cautious about is how much water may be gathering on the surface of your plants' leaves. Pooled water can cause fungus to breed and that will damage your foliage. In general, it's crucial that plants have good air circulation around them so that their leaf surfaces and pores stay healthy.

For a more consistent humidity solution, go for a humidifier, or use pebble trays, mini greenhouses, and/or healing boxes (see page 63).

11. **Is my plant dead?**

When you browse the plants at a store or see pictures of them on your social media feed, you're most likely seeing a plant at its peak. Like most living things, plants have growing cycles, so don't freak out if your plant doesn't always look like its green leafy self.

So, is your plant dead? There are excellent ways to tell if your plant has gone over to the other side. Funky smells and black and/or squishy roots (or none at all) are dead give-aways; if your plant has any of those symptoms, it might be time to say goodbye to your plant baby.

12. **Can I move my plant outdoors or indoors?**

One of the most significant differences between indoor and outdoor plants is that you can control the environment indoors by manipulating the light, temperature, and humid-ity. With outdoor plants, you need to be cognizant of your region and its weather.

Many plant parents like to put their indoor plants out-doors during the warmer months and then bring them back in when the weather starts to cool down. If you fall into that category, be sure to slowly acclimate your plants to their changed environment. For instance, if your plants experi-ence shock when coming back indoors, be sure to provide steady light and watering. Isolate them to rule out bringing any pests inside as well. If you suspect a plant has some hitchhikers, follow the steps on page 87. A great trick is to have a dedicated area for those specific outdoor plants that come indoors; that way they stay together, and you can set up a grow light to help keep them happy or at least stable until they return to the outdoors.

Pick a pot whose diameter is no more than 2 inches bigger than the present pot. You don't want to jump from a small pot to a pot that is too big because the extra potting medium can lead to too much moisture retention, which can rot the plant's root system.

1 Start by pouring your potting soil or medium into the base of the pot. If you are using a pot with a drainage hole, it's normal to have some of the medium come out of the hole. You can keep your work surface clean by laying down a tarp or some recycled newspaper.

2 Once you fill the pot about a quarter of the way full with the potting medium, place the plant in the pot. Hold it up to where you want your soil line, which is the same as where it was in the nursery pot.

3 While holding your plant centered in the pot, begin to pour (or scoop) the potting soil under and around the plant and roots. Be sure to go slowly so you don't cause any damage to the roots. Try not to bury the plant too deep in the soil—all that moisture could rot the stem.

4 If your plant is wobbly and won't stay upright, you can use a temporary trellis or stick to help stabilize it until the roots are established.

5 Give the average plant about a month to adjust, then check to see if it's established by gently tugging on it. If it pops up, the plant has not established roots in the new soil, but if your tug is met with resistance, that's good news.

PLANT PARENT QUIZ

My road to plant success wasn't all rainbows and sun-shine—it took some creative use of humidity, grow lights, and soil mixes! Getting in tune with your plants takes a lot of patience and a willingness to learn about the plants you decide to keep in your space. To understand plants and their personalities, you also have to understand who you are as a plant parent.

Throughout this guide, I address us all as "plant parents." And any parent will tell you that being responsible for a living thing is as rewarding as it is challenging! And there are as many types of plant parents as there are plants.

Admittedly, I've felt like each type of plant parent at some point over the years, and I think it's always a good idea to go plant shopping with a truthful idea of how much (or how little) work you want to commit to when it comes to caring for your plants. Plus, you can always come back to this quiz whenever you want to evaluate your style.

Take this fun quiz to help you assess your plant-parent personality. Answer these questions as truthfully as possible and add up your results to find your particular plant-parent personality. Keep in mind that there is no right way to be a plant parent! The most important thing is to know what works best for you and what makes you happiest.

QUESTION 1:

You're walking through a plant nursery and the first thing you do is:

1 POINT: Wonder how you ended up here.
2 POINTS: Ask the store clerk to help you choose a plant.
3 POINTS: Pick out all the plants you are going to buy for your friend's new apartment.
4 POINTS: Regret not taking a shopping cart because your hands are already full with five new plant babies.
5 POINTS: Admire the plants but realize you already have the majority that this nursery has to offer.

TOTAL POINTS SO FAR: _____

QUESTION 2:

You just purchased plants and brought them home. What do you do now?

1 POINT: Vibe with your plant and wonder if you should buy some more.
2 POINTS: Do meticulous research on your new plant.
3 POINTS: Rearrange all your other plants to make room for this new one. You also have already documented its entire journey from the plant store to your home.
4 POINTS: Isolate the plant, give it a name, show it around the apartment, and introduce it to its new plant family.
5 POINTS: Strictly isolate the plant for at least two weeks to rule out any bugs or issues that might affect the rest of your collection. You leave nothing to chance!

TOTAL POINTS SO FAR: _____

QUESTION 3:

You found a bug on your plant. You . . .

1 POINT: Didn't realize bugs could live on indoor plants.
2 POINTS: Try to identify what bug it is and how to treat it.
3 POINTS: Are personally insulted that your plant would do this to you and let the shop know their plants have bugs.
4 POINTS: Are already looking for a new place to live.
5 POINTS: Start meticulously cleaning the plant and your whole home.

TOTAL POINTS SO FAR: _____

QUESTION 4:

Something is wrong with your new plant, so now you . . .

1 POINT: Throw it out.
2 POINTS: Message a few people in your plant fam for advice and moral support.
3 POINTS: Cut off the bad leaves because that's not a cute look.
4 POINTS: Go into plant-savior mode and rescue that plant from death's door.
5 POINTS: Propagate in anticipation of the worst and try your best to reestablish the plant.

TOTAL POINTS SO FAR: _____

QUESTION 5:

A friend is hosting a plant swap; you bring . . .

1 POINT: Wine and cheese.

2 POINTS: A new baby plant you picked up from the store.

3 POINTS: A cutting from a plant you know no one has ever seen before but needs in their collection.

4 POINTS: A minimum of 10 cuttings you've been propagating.

5 POINTS: A few rare plants that you rooted and want to share because everyone should have a chance to grow some.

TOTAL POINTS SO FAR: _____

QUESTION 6:

A plant you've had for a long time is starting to look odd. You . . .

1 POINT: Wonder if you should replace it with a fake one so it never looks bad.

2 POINTS: Worry about whether you can keep it alive and think about maybe slowing down your plant purchases.

3 POINTS: Are already shopping for a new one.

4 POINTS: Freak out and think about all the things you might have done wrong.

5 POINTS: Try to analyze what might be wrong. You dig up the plant and look at its root health to assess the problem.

TOTAL POINTS SO FAR: _____

QUESTION 7:

A friend asks for plant advice. You . . .

1 POINT: Tell them to buy some faux plants so they don't have to worry about their plants dying.

2 POINTS: Link them to all your favorite plantstagrammers and/or shops with great information.

3 POINTS: Tell them to try new plants in the space and see how they do.

4 POINTS: Tell them about every single plant failure you've ever had and how not to make the same mistakes.

5 POINTS: Tell them to first look at the type of environment their space provides and then research the types of plants they want to buy.

TOTAL POINTS SO FAR: _____

QUESTION 8:

You would describe your plant collection as . . .

1 POINT: "Pretty Cool"

2 POINTS: "Lovely"

3 POINTS: "Trendy"

4 POINTS: "Perfect"

5 POINTS: "Never Finished"

TOTAL POINTS: _____

NOW THAT YOU HAVE YOUR TOTAL POINTS, CHECK TO SEE WHICH PLANT PARENT YOU ARE!

YOUR PLANT
PARENT
PERSONALITY
IS . . .

1–8 POINTS:

THE WORLD TRAVELER

❊ Thinks of plants more like decoration
❊ Never home enough to water the plants on a regular schedule
❊ Has considered switching to faux plants
❊ Knows plants by their common names
❊ Will water an already dead plant
❊ Might forget they even have plants

You're constantly on vacation mode, both physically and mentally. Maybe your busy schedule keeps you from remembering the leafy living things around your home, or you're just never home enough to keep an eye on them. Consider starting small with one or two plants to see if you can get into the groove of things. If you fall into this category, you are the perfect candidate for some of the "Ride or Die Plants" (page 94). It's a perfect place to start your plant journey; their ease of care will inspire your plant confidence.

I'VE BEEN THERE!

Checked out and too stressed and too busy to take care of the plants? When I run into these tougher times, I'm usually daydreaming about reducing my plant collection.

The biggest issue that gets in the way of my successfully growing plants is juggling many jobs and projects outside of my plant passion. There have been times when I've been so busy that even my boyfriend, Micah, notices the number of plants I've lost. It's definitely one way to test your plants' resilience! *But* it's not realistic if you want to keep plants in your space for the long term.

9–17 POINTS:

THE WORKIN' 9 TO 5

* Most common parent in the plant community
* Likes it when all the plants have the same care needs, like a designated watering day
* Doesn't sweat common things like a yellowing leaf every now and again (will even let yellowing leaves fall off on their own)
* Does basic research on what can and can't work in their environment
* Willing to buy a grow light if a plant needs it
* Doesn't choose favorites among their plant babies

Your weekends are scheduled with an itinerary of new plant shops you're going to visit. You love your new plant hobby and keep to a strict watering routine. You love learning new ways to care for them and are open to more plants but also understand your limits. You have your low-maintenance plant-care routine down pat and it's working like a well-oiled machine so you can enjoy your plants and all the good they bring to your home.

I'VE BEEN THERE!

Before I started to collect plants seriously, I was the Workin'
9 to 5 parent. I was casually bringing plants into my space
with only a basic knowledge about them. I didn't realize
plants had a lot more needs than I was fulfilling—I was just
hoping for the best.

18–26 POINTS:

THE DESIGNER

❋ Loves filling every empty shelf with some green
   plant babies
❋ Thinks of plants as an element of home decor
❋ Would rather keep plants that work well in the space
   rather than making adjustments for the plants
❋ Their space is loaded with all the Instagrammable
   essentials
❋ Totally has favorites
❋ Chooses plants based on their ease of care and
   general appearance
❋ Not into "rescuing that dying plant from [Big Brand
   Store]"

You love shopping for the "it" plant, and you already have the perfect spot for it in your home. The Designer plays the plant popularity game and really knows how to show off their favorites (the *Pilea peperomioides* is a perfect example).

You are constantly rearranging them to highlight their beauty and tend to get creative with different pots and thrifted items—anything to make your plants stand out! Placement and aesthetics are a priority for the Designer.

I'VE BEEN THERE!

I'll admit I've purchased a plant based solely on its looks and not on the care it needs. Sometimes you just can't resist those lush leaves, especially if it's #trending. But keep in mind your plant's needs when you're looking for that perfect spot! If it needs more light, maybe there's a windowsill that calls for a little touch of green.

27–35 POINTS:

THE HELICOPTER

* Removes yellow and brown crunchy leaves the minute they appear
* Names their plants but also knows their Latin names
* Loves cleaning plant leaves until they are shiny
* Willing to change their home environment to accommodate plant needs
* Isolates new plants to rule out any bugs before introducing them to the rest of the plant family
* Mistakes perlite for mealybugs and treats the entire collection *just in case*
* Hires a plant sitter while they're away
* Will turn any conversation into one about plants

Caring for plants can be an emotional roller coaster. Whether you have 3 or 300 plants, their well-being is your top priority. Most people have been this personality type at some point in their plant parenthood. Bringing home a new baby can feel overwhelming, and you want to be the best parent possible. You read all the books, take a class or two, and even alter your space for your new plant babies. You pay close attention to your collection, so you know the minute something goes wrong.

I'VE BEEN THERE!

I still, to this very day, find myself obsessing over my plant babies. When I started increasing my collection, I was constantly hovering over the plants, making sure they were still living or monitoring their health if they were on the decline. This plant personality still pops up every now and again, especially when I introduce a new plant baby to the fam. With enough plant confidence, this won't be the *only* plant parent you'll become.

36–44 POINTS:

THE COLLECTOR

* Interested in the plant's native home and environment
* Concerned about ethically sourcing plants
* Tends to have several of the same family of plants
* The home is more of a greenhouse
* Has several setups for growing and propagating
* Loves trading plants with other collectors, like Pokémon cards
* The majority of the collection is filled with rare or hard-to-find plants
* Easily distracted by topics discussing plants

You geek out over your plants. You're always seeking unique plants to keep in your home and you love watching them succeed. If the plants aren't doing well, you're not afraid to tackle the issue(s).

You may realize after a few happy houseplants that you are satisfied with what you have, and that you are more of an occasional plant buyer. Or you may realize there is no end in sight and you'll continuously search for beautiful plants to bring home. Being a Collector doesn't necessarily mean you've amassed a lot, but it does mean that you have favorite plant families and love collecting different species.

I'VE BEEN THERE!

It takes a long time to establish your plant collection. It took me a long time to feel like I had the plants I wanted in my space, with a plant-care routine I felt comfortable with. It takes a lot of balance and dedication, but it's worth it for the collection's success.

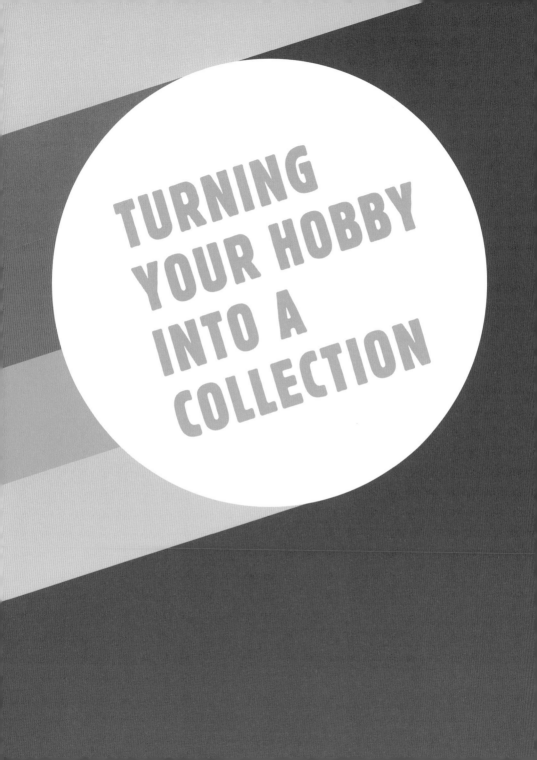

TURNING YOUR HOBBY INTO A COLLECTION

TIPS & TRICKS FOR HAPPY HOUSEPLANTS

Part of the fun of plant parenthood is experimenting and seeing what works or, sadly, what doesn't work. During this time of plant and parent matchmaking, it's surprising what each individual finds will work in their home. The best part of my own plant journey has been the experimental and essential tips and tricks I've picked up along the way that have made getting familiar with one's plants that much easier.

Here are some of my favorite tips for taking care of plants throughout the year; they will help take you from one plant to a whole collection.

GET TO KNOW YOUR ENVIRONMENT

Before committing to a plant, figure out the type of light your space provides. You can always download a compass app on your phone and find out which direction your windows face. What type of light is this plant receiving? The more light your plant receives typically means it's going to need to be watered more frequently—that is, less light, less water. (It's also why you should water more in the summer and less in the winter!)

You also want to be aware of any extreme conditions, like wide temperature changes. Is your space dry or humid, cold or hot? Maintaining a steady temperature is an essential part of houseplant care; extreme temperature shifts can shock your plants. The area's temperature can also determine how fast or slow the plants' soil dries out.

I keep my room temperatures fairly cool year-round to maintain that consistency, no matter the season. For plants that require heat or humidity, I cordon them off in separate areas so I can provide them with grow lights, heat mats, and/ or humidifiers.

When you buy plants, you'll notice that they typically are categorized by how much light they need. What do these categories mean?

BRIGHT LIGHT: This means your space receives anywhere from 5 to 8 hours of direct light (depending on the season) and is usually south or west facing. You can most likely see the sun for the majority of the day.

INDIRECT LIGHT: This refers to the room or space itself as being bright or full of light, without an exact visual of the sun. This can also sometimes describe east-facing light, like morning light, with no direct sun for the majority of the day. Similarly, it can describe the type of light that comes from southern and western exposures but away from the window and just in the open room. You would most likely see the sun for a bit, but even if you don't, the space is still bright.

LOW LIGHT: Most indoor spaces have low-light situations (think north facing). Low light can also be thought of as mainly shady. Many homes also experience low light during the winter months. In this situation, people most likely never see the sun directly.

1	2	3	4
SOUTH	**WEST**	**EAST**	**NORTH**
Bright light	Bright light in the morning	Indirect light in the morning	Low light
	Indirect light in the evening	Low light in the evening	

DO YOUR RESEARCH

When you decide to bring home a new plant, it's always a great idea to gather as much information on the plant as you can. Keep in mind that the care tips you get and read about are always starting points—every plant is individual. You will likely need to make adjustments based on your own specific space. But take it a step further and learn about where the plant lives in the wild. What is that habitat like? This paints a clear picture of what that plant might like emulated in your space—within reason, of course!

Choose the best pot

TERRA-COTTA WITH DRAINAGE: Terra-cotta is porous, allowing moisture to evaporate the quickest. It's a great option for plants that enjoy a more aerated root situation since terra-cotta is breathable. It's also an affordable option for most plants.

PLASTIC WITH DRAINAGE: Plastic pots are perfect for plants that need a bit more water retention because the plastic is not porous and thus holds the moisture longer. I love using plastic pots when I'm transitioning my water propagations into a soil medium.

CERAMIC WITHOUT DRAINAGE: These pots can be great for plants that need more moisture and humidity because the ceramic has been glazed, thus sealed. My favorite hack is to place my plant potted in a plastic pot with drainage inside a ceramic pot sitting on top of pebbles or hydro balls.

No matter what pot you choose, lay in a layer of small rocks, charcoal, sphagnum moss, and/or pebbles before adding your soil mix so as to encourage proper drainage and filtration. You should also be prepared to clean out the pots every six months to a year to ensure your plants are doing okay.

SIZE MATTERS: Another thing to consider when it comes to choosing pots is size. A large pot requires more soil and thus more moisture retention than a small pot. Picking the right pot size can be a game-changer. You want to be sure you're giving your plant a pot that is a maximum of 2 inches larger in diameter than it was in when you purchased it or that matches the plant size (including the plant's existing root system), whichever is bigger. If you ever feel unsure, it's always better to err on the smaller side. A large pot with a too-small plant puts your plant at risk of rotting because of all the extra soil medium that's present.

I'VE BEEN THERE!

There are lots of things I avoided doing when I started my plant-parent journey, including fertilizing my plants. I was intimidated by the whole idea of providing extra care, but once I gained enough plant confidence to *learn*, I realized it's really nothing more than reading directions on a bottle, measuring, and reminding myself that less is more! It made my plants happier and they grow at a more consistent pace.

ISOLATE YOUR PLANT: If you have a growing plant collection, isolate the newcomers to prevent infestation. Before bringing home the plant, inspect the leaves and soil and look at its overall health and appearance. Common pests to keep an eye out for are mealybugs, thrips, spider mites, whiteflies, aphids, and snails. If you think you spot some pests, identify them properly so you can find the best treatment. Most treatments involve cleaning and spraying the plant with items such as neem oil and other pest killers. It's common practice, if you do spot pests, to treat the plant every three to five days to be able to interrupt the bugs' life cycle. It can be frustrating, but this is also why it's good to keep new plants isolated until you can be certain they are pest free!

SELECT THE BEST POTTING MEDIUM: Depending on your plant's water needs, you should ask yourself what type of soil your plant will need to truly thrive. Most plants you purchase and bring home are in a generic soil medium. It took me a really long time before I felt confident enough to start mixing my own soils, but once I got the hang of it, I never went back. Now I have a base mix of charcoal and perlite; depending on the plant involved, I swap in other ingredients as necessary. See the "At-Home Soil Recipes" on page 69 to get your hands dirty and figure out what mixtures work best for your plants.

SUPERCHARGING A PLANT'S GROWTH: Let's talk about fertilizer! Potted indoor plants are limited to the nutrients you provide in that initial soil. Most soils have tiny bits of fertilizer to help jump-start your plant's growth, but after a while, the plant will deplete those nutrients, which can stunt growth and even diminish a plant's health. Refreshing the soil with fertilizer or nutrients ensures that your plants will continue to thrive.

There are types of fertilizers, natural and synthetic, that come in different forms: powder, liquid, and pellets, which can be found online or in stores. Start with an easily accessible fertilizer and test it on a few plants. Most important, be careful not to be heavy-handed. Overfertilizing your plant can result in "fertilizer burn," which is just as bad as it sounds. Follow the directions listed on the package to avoid overfertilizing.

Remember, even though you want to ensure that you feed your plants during the growing season (typically the warmer months), you still want to provide some food for your plants during the colder months as well. Since indoor plants pretty much grow all year round, they will happily take the nutrients.

DON'T LET YOUR COLLECTION OVERWHELM YOU: It's totally normal to phase in and out of plant trends. It's also normal to find that some plants that used to bring you joy just don't do it for you anymore. If you feel you've "over-collected" some plants, it may be time to clean out your plant "closet." Take the opportunity to sell your healthy plants to parents just starting out or donate them to nurseries, friends, family, neighbors, schools, community gardens, or local businesses! A good way to keep your collection fresh and manageable is to practice the "one in, one out" method. This means that for every plant you buy, you get rid of one.

HUMIDITY 101: IT'S A JUNGLE IN HERE!

Living in a dry environment doesn't mean you can't have tropical plants in your collection. A creative mix of humidifiers, glass domes, clear plastic boxes, pebble trays, and mini greenhouses can keep plants happy year-round, even in the dead of winter when homes are heated and quite dry. Most tropical plants rely on moisture from the air, so it's important to wipe down the surfaces of the leaves (see page 67) to keep them looking lush and plump within their special containers. You also want to monitor the condensation: dry off any pools of water that may gather on the leaves using a gentle cloth or reusable paper towel.

It's also good to give these plants a break in humidity. Air circulation is just as refreshing and important for the plants as it is for us. For plants that need consistent high humidity (like anthuriums), consider finding a vessel or enclosure, like a dome or cache, to put them in so they can create their own humidity.

If you don't have the means or space to use any of the following hacks, you can have success by grouping together a lot of plants to increase the humidity—community building at its finest!

HUMIDIFIER

My apartment jungle relies on three humidifiers to keep my collection lush. Not every plant parent will need to have this many humidifiers running constantly, but I find they make a world a difference, especially during the winter.

If this is your choice, look for a humidifier that provides both cool and warm mist. Warm mist in the winter is like a warm hug for me and my plants, whereas the cool mist is a refreshing breeze in the hot summer months. Also, look for something with a fairly large tank so you don't have to refill it multiple times a day.

GREEN RULE OF THUMB

CLEANING YOUR HUMIDIFIER REGULARLY IS IMPORTANT BECAUSE THE TANK AND THE IMMEDIATE AREA ARE SUSCEPTIBLE TO BACTERIAL AND MOLD GROWTH. MY GO-TO METHOD IS TO SOAK THE TANK IN HOT WATER AND WHITE VINEGAR AND SCRUB IT WITH CITRIC ACID. DEPENDING ON HOW FRE-QUENTLY YOU USE YOUR HUMIDIFIER, CLEANING IT ONCE EVERY TWO WEEKS OR ONCE A MONTH IS RECOMMENDED.

PEBBLE TRAY: A pebble tray is a great, low-maintenance way to increase the humidity around a plant. You can do something as simple as filling the bottom of a ceramic or decorative pot (with no drainage hole) with rocks. Then place the smaller nursing or plastic pot with the plant in it on top. When you water the plant and the water drains out the bottom, it will fill the pebble tray and act as a humidity-producing source for the plant. You can also set the pot atop the pebble tray (with a lip) and fill the tray with water.

GREEN RULE OF THUMB

ANYTIME YOU'RE DEALING WITH MOISTURE, BE CAREFUL NOT TO WET YOUR SURROUNDING FURNITURE. A GREAT TRICK IS TO PROTECT THE FURNITURE WITH A PLASTIC TABLECLOTH. I DON'T RECOMMEND PLACING YOUR HUMIDI-FIER ON OR NEAR EXPENSIVE OR BELOVED FURNITURE, EITHER. YOU NEVER KNOW WHEN SOMETHING MIGHT LEAK.

HEALING BOX: With an apt name, the healing box has brought back many of my plants from the brink of death.

In short, a healing box is a closed, clear plastic box that you keep plants in, helping promote growth through high humidity. The condensation that gathers on the inside walls provides ample humidity for the plants within. If you're interested in going this route, find a large, clear storage box with a lid; these are sold at any home goods store and come with grow lights. The lid locks the moisture in and the grow lights encourage more growth. Make sure to remove the top once a week so the plants receive fresh air; you can even set up a mini fan to help increase air circulation. Water the plants in the box once a month and clean it regularly. You can remove the plants once you feel they have grown or healed sufficiently. If you're using the healing box for propagation, they're ready when the plant roots have grown at least 1 to 2 inches long.

MINI GREENHOUSE: If you have the space and want something a bit larger and more permanent for your plants, you can invest in a mini greenhouse to provide a home with a steady high moisture level—it's basically a giant healing box. A mini greenhouse normally is made with metal or plastic piping that forms the foundation, and plastic shelves form the walls. This setup is a little bit more involved, as you need to maintain the environment inside the greenhouse, big or small, with fans, grow lights, and a humidifier.

WINTER CARE

t's normal to struggle with indoor plants during the colder months. The leaves yellow, growth might slow down, and some won't make it through the dark times. Depending on where you are in the world, winter can be rough on indoor plants. As long as you can meet your plants' primary needs (light, water, good soil, and humidity), they should have no problems, no matter the season.

Here's how to help your plants weather the cold.

TEMPERATURE: Extreme changes in temperature can damage leaves and shock your plants. Normal signs of shock are yellow-ing leaves and leaf loss. As with a fish, you can't throw a plant into a new environment and expect it to thrive; it needs time to acclimate. If you can, keep your plants at the same temperature or within a small temperature range year-round, and keep them away from windows and doors. If some plants require warm temperatures to encourage growth, consider buying a heat mat specially made for plants.

LIGHT: The first thing I like to do is set up grow lights through-out my space so as to provide more light. I use both the red-blue spectrum lights and the white full-spectrum lights. Plants react differently to different types of light, so you want to cover all your bases. You might also rearrange some of your plants to give them the most light possible. Pay attention to how the light changes in your home and how your plants handle it. For instance, look for the time your light is the strongest and how the sunlight moves around your space. These are great factors to keep in mind, especially when you are plant placing. Generally, when you're finding the right spot for your plants, the hope is that it is each plant's permanent thriving spot—but only time and attention will tell which spot is the best.

HUMIDITY: Providing humidity for your plants during the winter can really make the difference between losing and saving them. When the temperature drops and plants slow their growth, mistakes can happen. Overwatering and cold drafts are the top killers during the winter.

CLEANING: You read that right! Keeping your plants clean is important year-round. Be sure to dust the leaves (which you should do in every season) to keep their pores clear, making it easier to capture the light and photosynthesize. Use a damp gentle cloth to clean and wipe the surfaces. I prefer mixing a few drops of neem oil with a little bit of peppermint castile soap and water. I then take a cotton ball and wipe down the leaves front and back, and even down the stems. Caution: Never use the same cleaning material from plant to plant, or else clean your cloth between plant cleansings. For fragile leaves (like velvet-textured ones), be very gentle and opt for just water and light drops of castile soap.

REPOTTING: As the chilly weather rolls in, taking care of your plants may mean repotting. If you think a plant is rootbound (do you see roots stretching out the drainage hole?), then repot that plant in a pot that is no larger than 2 inches in diameter than its current pot. A tip: Place the pot your plant is in now inside the pot you want to move it to. If the empty space between the two pots is more than 2 inches, that pot is too large (see page 29). And when repotting, take the opportunity to look at the health of the plant's roots. Usually, you want to see nice white roots. Give it fresh soil (which adds fresh nutrients) just in time for winter and set it back into place.

PROPAGATION: At the start of winter, you might consider taking a few cuttings, just as an insurance policy! If you think you may have some issues with a plant or are just scared it might be dying, taking cuttings or offsets (be sure you know how that plant propagates) will save you the pain of a total loss.

WATERING: In winter, receiving less light means your plants aren't photosynthesizing as actively. As a result, they don't need as much water or fertilizer. If you water too much, you can open your plant up to root rot because the roots won't absorb as much moisture in this more dormant state. This doesn't mean stop watering—just cut back!

GREEN RULE OF THUMB

IF YOU NOTICE A PLANT STRUGGLING TO PUSH OUT A NEW LEAF, CONSIDER FERTILIZING THE PLANT. THE ENERGY BOOST WILL KEEP THAT NEW LEAF FROM BECOMING STUNNED OR DEFORMED.

AT-HOME SOIL RECIPES

E veryone uses a little something different here and there, but a great starting point when it comes to potting mediums is a mix of potting soil, perlite, and charcoal. Play around with the proportions based on the plant you're potting and whether it will benefit more from a light and airy mix (flushes throughout the soil and roots and out of the drainage hole) or more from a moisture-retaining mixture (water still flushes through but components help retain some moisture within the soil). Good plants start with good soil, so make sure what you are using is new and full of nutrients.

GREEN RULE OF THUMB

STORE YOUR SOIL IN AN AIRTIGHT CONTAINER IN A COOL, DRY SPACE. MOIS-
TURE CAN ATTRACT FUNGUS AND GNATS, WHICH ARE THE LAST THINGS YOU
WANT IN YOUR SOIL.

There are lots of materials you can use to mix soil, but here is a list of common, easy-to-find ingredients that plant parents can mix to create their own soil mixtures:

POTTING SOIL: Garden soil that contains fresh nutrients for your plant and sometimes fertilizer. You can purchase this in bags.

PERLITE: Ground volcanic rock that holds moisture and fluffs up and puts air into your mix. This allows more water to pass through when you're watering that plant. You can also use vermiculite, which is a ground mineral product, but I'm a perlite girl, personally!

CHARCOAL: Like perlite, ground charcoal creates an airier medium. It also improves the quality of your soil by allowing air to flow through and creates pores that help hold nutrients for your plants. Plus, it's great for avoiding harmful fungus and bacteria.

ORCHID BARK/CHIPS: These are perfect for breaking up the soil and providing more air circulation for the roots of these air plants. I also find some roots love attaching themselves to the chunks of bark, making the roots stronger and happier.

COCONUT COIR: Ground coconut husks are similar to peat moss and provide a great texture to the soil, as well as retains moisture. Coco coir tends to expand when watered, so be aware when you're using it in a pot; you want to leave some room at the top of the pot for that expansion.

SPHAGNUM MOSS: Bits of sphagnum moss are excellent at holding moisture once it is rehydrated. I love breaking the strands of moss into smaller pieces and then adding them to my soil mix. It's ideal for plants that would benefit from more moisture retention.

SAND: Coarse sand, like builder's sand, filters the water but retains some moisture, providing a nice balance for plants. By creating its own drainage system, sand is great at filtering moisture in the pot, and it's perfect for creating aerated soil so that roots can obtain oxygen.

HYDROBALLS (AKA LECCA BALLS OR CLAY BALLS): These are lightweight clay balls that are popularly used as a terrarium substrate but also have garden applications. I find that plant roots like to adhere to them, and they are wonderful for water propagation, helping to create a sturdier plant root system.

SOIL TOPPERS: These are a great option for aesthetics. I love topping off a plant's soil to help give it a cohesive look among my many plants. Some of my favorite toppers are orchid bark or orchid chips, HydroBalls, lava rocks, pebbles, and sand. Sand is also a great option if you're experiencing fungus gnats, as it acts as a natural deterrent.

GREEN RULE OF THUMB

TEST YOUR SOIL MIXTURES BY SQUEEZING SOME IN THE PALM OF YOUR HAND. FOR LIGHT AND AIRY MIXES, THE SOIL SHOULD CRUMBLE AND LOSE ITS SHAPE. FOR MOISTURE-RETAINING SOILS, IT SHOULD BE A LITTLE CRUMBLY BUT KEEP SOME OF ITS FORM.

SOIL RECIPE CARDS

While I give some idea of measurements here, once you start to understand what your plants need and want from you and your space, you'll be able to adjust your potting medium without reference to them. The proportions (parts) in these recipe cards are just suggestions; you can customize the mix for each plant. But until then, here are some places to start.

GREEN RULE OF THUMB

GRAB A LARGE PLASTIC CONTAINER WITH A LID AND MAKE A BIG BATCH OF "FIRST DATE" SOIL, AS IT'S A GREAT BASE FOR MOST HOUSEPLANTS. DEPENDING ON THE PLANT, USE THIS MIX AS THE BASE AND ADD WHATEVER ELSE YOU NEED. THIS IS ALSO A GREAT WAY TO START SO THAT MIXING YOUR OWN MEDIUM DOESN'T FEEL SO OVERWHELMING.

FIRST DATE MIX

Like any good first date, here is a great soil recipe to start off with if you are just getting the hang of mixing your own medium. This soil mix drains well, but it retains enough moisture to be a great option for most houseplants.

1	part potting soil
½	part perlite
½	part charcoal
¾	part orchid chips or bark

LEAF LOVER MIX

This mix is airy, drains well, and is perfect for philodendrons, monstera, and most other foliage-filled houseplants. I added coco coir and sphagnum moss for a little bit of added moisture.

1	part potting soil	¼	part coconut coir
¾	part perlite	¼	part chopped sphagnum
¾	part charcoal		moss
1	part orchid chips		

SWEETHEART MIX

This soil mix drains well and retains moisture, so it's perfect for anthuriums and alocasia. The mix is great for plants that have roots that like airflow but also love that extra bit of moisture that can be retained in the sphagnum moss.

1	part sphagnum moss	½	part orchid chips
¼	part HydroBalls	¼ - ½	part charcoal
¼	part orchid bark	¼	part potting soil

HUGGABLE MIX

This mix is airy, chunky, and drains well, and is perfect for monstera, anthuriums, philodendrons, cacti, and succulents. With lots of chunky medium in the mix, the roots can't resist latching on. This is great for plants with large roots.

1¼	part potting soil	½	part perlite
½	part HydroBalls	¾	part charcoal
½	part orchid bark	¾	part orchid chips

DESERT DARLING MIX

This mix drains well and is perfect for cacti and succulents.
The mix is also great for plants that have finer, thinner root systems.

1	part potting soil
¾	part perlite
½	part charcoal
½	part sand
¼	part orchid chips

WHAT IS PROPAGATION AND HOW DO I DO IT?

Propagation is the process of reproducing or multiplying plants from a mother plant. These can be done by taking cuttings of offshoots.

This is one of my favorite aspects of collecting plants! Plants propagate in different ways, so not all plants can be cut to propagate. A quick internet search typically does the trick to determine how your particular plant propagates. Whether you're growing your plant collection, gifting them to friends and family, saving a dying plant, or building your plant confidence by adding a new skill, here are some steps and my favorite ways to propagate.

TYPES OF PROPAGATION

Division from offsets or pups

I find this to be one of the easiest ways to propagate. The primary, or mama plant, will produce little offsets (babies), which you can then separate at the root. The best way to take the cuttings is to unpot the plant, clear the soil off the base, and use a pair of clean shears or a knife to make a cut (horizontally, side to side) about 1 inch down the baby plant's main stem, allowing the pup to have some roots.

You want to take as much plant from the mother as possible so your baby has a good chance of success. I also suggest waiting until the offset has grown 2 to 3 inches before removing it from its mama. Think of the offsets as still being attached to the mother's umbilical cord: You want to make sure the mother supplies it with enough nutrients for the baby plant to grow strong after you separate them.

After you cut your pup, you can place it in the soil or in moist sphagnum moss, or use a water propagation method (see page 80).

Cuttings

This propagation type is when you take clean shears and cut under a node or knuckle of a plant. From there, you can pop those cuttings into water, wrap them with sphagnum moss, or use a combination of water and HydroBalls, or water and perlite. When propagating with cuttings, you want to encourage new root growth. Once those new roots have grown 2 to 3 inches long, you can put the cuttings into soil. Keep the soil on the moist side for two weeks, then continue by meeting the plant's natural care needs.

Leaf propagation

This method is when you remove a healthy leaf from a plant and use it to grow new plants. You can either cut or pluck the leaf off the mother plant and place it on the surface of potting soil or on a layer of sphagnum moss. If it works, the original leaf will shrivel up and the new offsets will grow.

Air layering

This is when you wrap a medium, like moist sphagnum moss, around the node or knuckle of a plant. You then tape cling wrap around it to enclose the moss around the knuckle. After a few weeks, the knuckle will have sprouted roots, and then you can cut beneath the node and pot your newly rooted plant. Remember, you're not cutting anything off until those roots grow from the

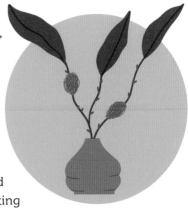

node. This way, you are taking advantage of that node, hoping for it to root while it's still attached to the mother plant.

I'VE BEEN THERE!

When I first started collecting, I was a little daunted by the idea of propagation, but knowing how to do it saved my collection when it was nearly devastated by mealybugs.

WAYS TO PROPAGATE

Water

One of my favorite ways to propagate plants is with water. You start with a tall, thin vessel, fill it with distilled water, add the cutting or offset, then put the vessel in a spot with bright, indirect light. Grouping the cuttings from the same plant in a jar together can help stimulate quicker root growth.

As the water evaporates, be sure to top it off with more distilled H_2O—never change the water. If the water is green, that's actually a good thing; that algae in the water will supply some added nutrients to encourage root growth. The only time you might need to consider changing the water and cleaning the vessel is if the water turns reddish and has an odor, indicating rot. If the rot hasn't affected a lot of the cutting, you might be able to remove the rotting section and keep the rest; put it in fresh water to keep its growth on track.

It's best to wait for at least 2 inches of root growth before you transfer any cuttings to a soil medium. And when you do the transfer, keep the soil on the moist side for the first two weeks while the plant gets used to its new medium. Don't be shocked if your baby starts to look bad; it'll look worse before it gets better! Also, remember to clean your vessel(s) between use.

GREEN RULE OF THUMB

HYDROBALLS ARE ALSO A GREAT TOOL FOR PROPAGATING PLANTS. PLAC-ING THE CUTTINGS IN A MIXTURE WITH HYDROBALLS WILL HELP ESTAB-LISH STRONG, HEALTHY ROOTS BECAUSE THE EMERGING ROOTS CAN ATTACH THEMSELVES TO THE BALLS FOR STABILITY.

Sphagnum moss

I love using moss to propagate plants. This method keeps the propagating medium moist and helps create a stable root system. You can find blocks of dehydrated sphagnum moss online. When you receive the block, crumble a handful or two into a bowl and add water to rehydrate the moss. Then place the wet sphagnum in a nursing pot with your cutting. I also like to break apart the long pieces of sphagnum, easily ripping them with my hands.

Soil

Sometimes you can place your cuttings directly into your soil medium. If that's the case, keep the soil on the damp side, not allowing it to dry out in between waterings, and provide bright, indirect light. You can switch to a normal watering routine once the cutting is established. Two ways to tell if your cutting has successfully rooted is to look for new growth emerging; alternatively, you can gently tug on the plant in the nursing pot and see if it gives some resistance.

WHEN YOU TRANSFER YOUR WATER-PROPAGATED CUTTINGS TO SOIL, KEEP YOUR NEW PLANT ON THE MOIST SIDE FOR A WHILE. IT'S NORMAL FOR THE YOUNG PLANT TO EXPERIENCE SHOCK WHEN IT'S TRANSFERRED TO SOIL. IT MIGHT LOOK WORSE BEFORE IT GETS BETTER! JUST MONITOR THE PLANT AND BE PATIENT WHILE ITS ROOTS ESTABLISH THEMSELVES IN THE POTTING MEDIUM.

Plastic box

This method (sometimes called "butterfly propagation") involves using a clear plastic box and sphagnum moss. You lay the cuttings on top of the moist moss and seal the box to trap in the moisture. Using individual pots of sphagnum in the plastic box allows you to root many plants at once. This is typically helpful when propagating plants with many nodes; the knuckle-shaped parts of the stem sprouts roots along a line, like a string of hearts.

HOW TO LOOK FOR A HEALTHY PLANT— IRL

Plant shopping—in real life—is so much fun! You are surrounded by tons of gorgeous greenery, with the hope of bringing home a brand-new plant baby to join your plant family. With all those options, how can you be sure you're making the right choice?

Here are a few tips.

ASK QUESTIONS

When you find a plant that you love, ask a member of the staff what the name of the plant is and what general care information they might have for it. If they don't know, you can always do a quick online search. Try to get a good sense of whether this plant is one you can work with.

INSPECT THE PLANT

Check the overall look of the plant. Avoid plants with many damaged leaves (holes, spotting, brown or yellow areas) because there could be a fungus present. Look for pests or anything moving around. Check the top and undersides of the leaves for movement, webbing, or anything hiding in where the leaves attach to the stems. You want to bring plants home, not pests. Look for signs of any rot or decay (looks black or feels mushy on the stem).

CHOOSE GROWTH

I like choosing plants with already a fair amount of growth or offsets. If a plant looks like it has a new leaf emerging, or babies in the pot, that means it's a healthy and active plant.

BRING IT HOME

Isolate your new plant baby, and provide it with fresh soil and a clean pot. Remember, you're taking that plant from a nursery where there were optimal plant conditions and placing it in your new environment. It is common for a new plant to experience shock, so it might get worse before it gets better. Give your plant a chance to bounce back before you call it quits!

PLANT-CARE ROUTINE

Establishing a plant-care routine is really important, but the task can sometimes feel overwhelming. My solution is to break up my routine into daily, weekly, and monthly duties. No matter how you organize yourself, it's just important to keep a manageable and consistent schedule. Designating certain tasks for daily, weekly, and monthly events makes plant parenting a whole lot easier!

DAILY DANCE: This routine is usually the easiest and most enjoyable part of caring for plants. Give your babies a scan: Look at the foliage, check the soil for dehydration, and keep an eye out for pests. Your daily routine is really about taking a general survey of how the plants are doing and making mental notes for what you might need to do during your weekly or monthly maintenance.

WEEKLY WALKTHROUGH: This routine typically involves watering! Once to twice a week, depending on the season, I water my plants. I also schedule when to give my plants nutrients or take them into the shower for a rinse. My weekly walkthrough, besides watering, also consists of checking up on propagations, examining healing or recovering plants, and looking in on new or isolated plants. During this time, I'm really getting a chance to see how each plant is doing in its soil and pot. I normally make a list of plants I'll need to pull for monthly maintenance.

MONTHLY MAINTENANCE: This is when I get down and dirty with my plant projects. This routine normally consists of repotting plants, checking root health, assessing or treating a pest issue, and monthly cleaning. During monthly maintenance, I also change plant placements and see if some plants would do better in other areas of my apartment. I also check on any plants in my healing box to see if they are ready to be brought out into the apartment. Overall, the monthly maintenance is more complicated based on what my daily and weekly routines tell me.

HARRY, THE HITCHHIKER

When I purchased my variegated monstera variety named Thai Constellation from eBay, it traveled from Florida to New York. I was so worried about stressing the plant further that I left it in its nursing pot and original soil. Even though the plant was fine, when I finally went to repot it, I discovered an anole (a very small lizard that's native to Florida) living at the bottom of the pot! Harry, as I named him, was living off the roots of the plant and the water I had given it. So what I'm saying is, you really want to check your new plant carefully and maybe change that soil. I've said it before, but I'll say it again: Check your new babies thoroughly and always repot them if you can.

THE
PLANT
DATING
SCENE

aring for plants is such a rewarding experience! And a big part of the fun is bringing home new babies. There will be times when a plant you love just doesn't work for you and your home, but there are also other times when a plant surprises you and meshes well with you and your life (for me, that meshing was the snake plant). In other words, this guide is a starting point, and, while I include each plant's ideal conditions, that doesn't mean it's the only way to care for them or that a particular plant *won't* work for you.

Think of this guide as you would a plant-dating app. Once you decide on a match, you and your plant will meet and see if there is potential for a long-term relationship. If it's not a perfect pairing, no worries! Come back and try again.

The good news is that there are so many plants available on the market today. Plant parents have spoken and demanded variety, and growers have responded. Indeed, there are so many options you can find in person, and exploring what's out there and searching for new plants are part of the fun! You never know when you'll have a spontaneous connection with a particular plant.

I guarantee that there is at least one plant out there that will make you want to swipe right—whether it's based on appearance or care regimen. Remember, everyone's plant journey will be different. It's all about making adjustments and discovering what fits best with your lifestyle and environment.

Happy growing!

GREEN RULE OF THUMB

PLANT TAXONOMY CAN BE A BIT DIFFICULT TO KEEP UP WITH, ESPECIALLY WITH CATEGORY CHANGES AND NEW DISCOVERIES ALWAYS BEING MADE. TRY YOUR BEST TO ID YOUR PLANT, EVEN IF THE NAME LISTED HERE NO LONGER MATCHES. THIS WILL REALLY HELP YOU TO UNDERSTAND AND CONNECT WITH YOUR PLANTS.

A QUICK KEY FOR THRIVING PLANTS

LIGHT

* ❋ Low light: Plants that can tolerate shady conditions
* ❋ Indirect light: A bright room, with little to no direct exposure to the sun
* ❋ Bright light: Southern or western exposure, meaning the space receives anywhere from 5 to 8 hours of direct light (you can most likely see the sun)

WATER

* ❋ Water regularly: Keep your plant on a schedule and wait for the soil to dry between waterings
* ❋ Soaking: Fill up a sink or container with room temperature water and submerge the plant's drainage hole for 10 to 20 minutes
* ❋ Drought tolerant: Allow more time to pass between waterings; these can be less schedule-based

HUMIDITY

* ❋ Low: Humidity level below 40 percent
* ❋ Normal: The natural humidity level of your space, typically 40 to 60 percent humidity
* ❋ High: Humidity at 60 to 90 percent

AIRFLOW

* ❋ Normal: The natural airflow in your space
* ❋ High: Use a fan or open window to augment airflow

TEMPERATURE

* ❋ Normal: The natural temperature of your space, typically 68 to 72 degrees

✳ Warm: A warmer than average environment, from 72 to 86 degrees
✳ Hot: An environment of 86 to 100 degrees, which is typically achieved by being in direct sun or using an electronic heating mat

GREEN RULE OF THUMB

I GROW MY <u>ALOCASIA CUPREA</u> IN SPHAGNUM MOSS (INSTEAD OF SOIL) AND PLACE IT IN BRIGHT TO BRIGHT INDIRECT SUN WITH NORMAL TO HIGH HUMIDITY. MY FRIEND IN FLORIDA GROWS THIS SAME PLANT IN FULL SHADE, IN A SOIL MIX, AND WITH HIGH HUMIDITY. SOMETIMES, YOU HAVE TO MAKE ADJUSTMENTS AND WORK WITH WHAT YOU HAVE AND APPLY WHAT WORKS BEST FOR THAT PLANT IN YOUR SPACE. IN OTHER WORDS, CARE ALMOST ALWAYS VARIES FROM ENVIRONMENT TO ENVIRONMENT, AT LEAST TO SOME DEGREE.

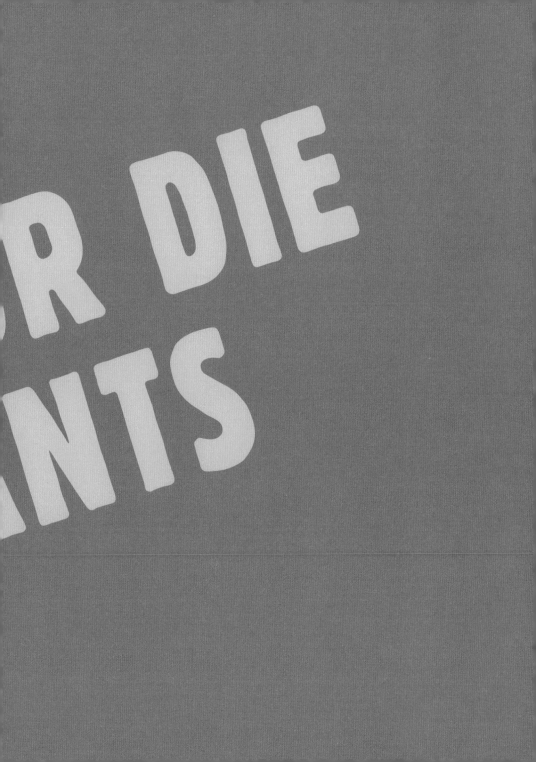

While your plant journey can start with any type of plant you buy, these plants are hard to kill and can do wonders for your plant confidence.

Like any living thing, plants have their essential needs, but these leafy little babies can tolerate any number of mistakes that might come with being a new plant in your home. They are forgiving, much like you should be to yourself, as you build your plant knowledge.

THE PEACEMAKER

JADE PLANT
(Crassula ovata)

BEST PAIRED WITH THESE PLANT PARENTS

The World Traveler
The Workin' 9 to 5

SOIL RECIPE

Desert Darling Mix

PROFILE

This stress-free plant is a great intro plant for any newbie. Owing to its thick, trunk-like branches and bonsai appeal, the jade succulent provides any home with a peaceful vibe. They are also easy prop-agators, making it effortless to start a whole new plant. Provide it with a bright sunny spot and balance out your water-ing by allowing the soil to dry out before watering it again. Try not to allow the leaves to shrivel, but if they do, this is a big sign that your plant is asking for some much-needed H_2O. Respecting its basic needs will ensure you will have this plant for generations to come.

THRIVING CONDITIONS

Light — Bright, indirect

Water — Regular (drought tolerant during winter)

Humidity — Normal

Airflow — Normal

Temperature — Normal to warm

Pet Friendly — No

Native — South Africa

THE SUPPORTIVE FRIEND

WATERMELON PEPEROMIA

(*Peperomia argyreia*)

BEST PAIRED WITH THESE PLANT PARENTS

The Workin' 9 to 5
The Designer
The Helicopter

SOIL RECIPE

First Date Mix
Leaf Lover Mix
Desert Darling Mix

PROFILE

Cheering you into early plant parenthood is the beautiful peperomia. This understanding and easy-to-propagate plant is excellent for new plant parents looking to diversify their leaf varieties. Along with being pet friendly, the plant's succulentlike leaves call for a lower maintenance routine—as in, it will forgive you if you forget to water it. Since the peperomia comes in a variety of colors and textures, you can create an entire cheer squad just for yourself at home.

THRIVING CONDITIONS

Light — Bright to indirect

Water — Regular

Humidity — Normal to high

Airflow — Normal to high

Temperature — Normal to warm

Pet Friendly — Yes

Native — South America

THE PARTIER

ZZ PLANT
(*Zamioculcas zamiifolia*)

BEST PAIRED WITH THESE PLANT PARENTS

The Workin' 9 to 5
The World Traveler

SOIL RECIPE

First Date Mix
Leaf Lover Mix

PROFILE

They are the established partygoers, bringing you to all the best ragers. They help you skip the line and take you straight to the front of your plant parent A-game. The ZZ plant, with its lush, green leaves, is a showstopper that can tolerate even the lowest of lights. It's easygoing and easy growing, making it the perfect plant to party on for a lifetime in your collection.

GREEN RULE OF THUMB

FOR PLANTS WITH FLEXIBLE CARE, YOU WANT TO BALANCE THE LIGHT AND THE WATER. REMEMBER: MORE LIGHT TENDS TO MEAN MORE WATER AND VICE VERSA. SO IF YOU HAVE YOUR PLANT IN A LOW-LIGHT SITUATION, YOU CAN WATER IT LESS FREQUENTLY.

THRIVING CONDITIONS

Light —— Low or bright to indirect

Water —— Drought tolerant

Humidity —— Normal

Airflow —— Normal

Temperature —— Normal

Pet Friendly —— No

Native —— West Africa

THE BOLD ONE

SNAKE PLANT OR MOTHER-IN-LAW'S TONGUE

(*Dracaena trifasciata*, formerly *Sansevieria trifasciata*)

BEST PAIRED WITH THESE PLANT PARENTS

The World Traveler
The Workin' 9 to 5
The Designer
The Helicopter

SOIL RECIPE

First Date Mix
Leaf Lover Mix
Desert Darling Mix

PROFILE

Like Rocky or the Karate Kid, the snake plant is the hero you didn't know you needed. With its resilient attitude and a look that always feels familiar, it's the plant you never really noticed until—BAM!—it has turned your *house* into a *home*. This friendly face might be a slow grower in lower light, but give it optimal conditions and watch the tall leaves become the talk of the town.

THRIVING CONDITIONS

Light —— Low or bright, indirect

Water —— Regular (drought tolerant during winter)

Humidity —— Normal

Airflow —— Normal

Temperature —— Normal

Pet Friendly —— No

Native —— Western Africa

THE PLANT NEXT DOOR

POTHOS OR DEVIL'S IVY

(*Epipremnum aureum*)

**BEST PAIRED
WITH THESE
PLANT PARENTS**

The Workin' 9 to 5
The Designer
The Helicopter

SOIL RECIPE

First Date Mix
Leaf Lover Mix

PROFILE

With enough patterns to satisfy everyone, this classic beauty happily hangs long and free from a top shelf. My favorite way to style it is to use clear Command hooks to encourage growth along my walls. Kind and compassionate for the beginner enthusiast, this unassuming plant might surprise you by becoming lush and abundant, quickly claiming room in your heart and transforming your space into an unexpected paradise.

THRIVING CONDITIONS

Light — Bright, indirect

Water — Regular

Humidity — Normal to high

Airflow — Normal

Temperature — Normal

Pet Friendly — No

Native — Solomon Islands

THE ADVENTURER

AIR PLANTS

(*Tillandsia* spp.)

BEST PAIRED WITH THESE PLANT PARENTS

The Workin' 9 to 5
The Helicopter

SOIL RECIPE

None

PRO TIP

ALLOW THESE BABIES
TO DRY UPSIDE DOWN
ON A TOWEL AFTER
THEIR WEEKLY SOAK.

PROFILE

At the tippy top of the easy plant list is the tillandsia group. These daring epiphytes, growing on the surface of other plants, may throw you for a loop. Available in an array of styles, they don't require repotting or planting, and they have primary care needs that can easily be met by any plant parent. Their easy care makes them like the adventurer who is always ready to move. These air plants love a long soak and like to have air between their leaves, just as a traveler doesn't need soil to thrive and instead lives off moisture and fresh air. Meet their simple needs, and they'll reward you with generations of one-of-a-kind plants.

THRIVING CONDITIONS

Light — Bright, indirect

Water — Soaking

Humidity — Normal to high

Airflow — High

Temperature — Normal to warm

Pet Friendly — Yes

Native — North, Central, and South America

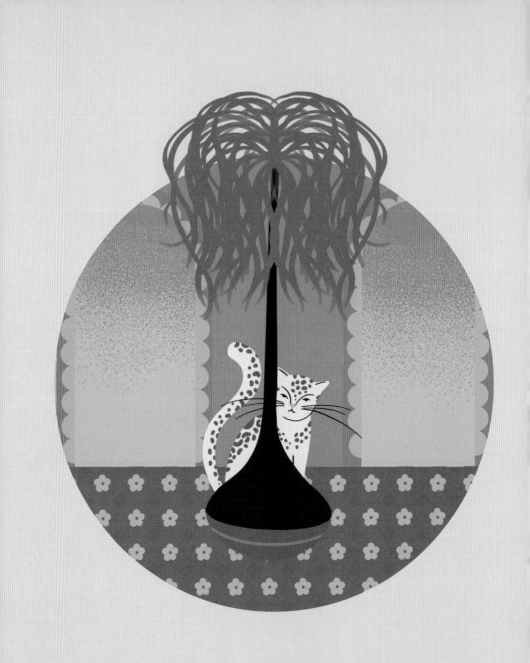

THE TRICKSTER

PONYTAIL PALM
(*Beaucarnea recurvata*)

BEST PAIRED WITH THESE PLANT PARENTS

The Workin' 9 to 5
The Designer

SOIL RECIPE

First Date Mix
Desert Darling Mix

PROFILE

Despite its nickname and look, this plant is not actually a palm; rather, it is a member of the agave family and is a succulent in disguise. And while the name may be deceiving, its care is not. Its treelike trunk stores water, making it perfect for the laid-back plant parent. Give this trickster some bright sunshine, and it will push out some curly hairlike leaves for you to enjoy.

THRIVING CONDITIONS

Light —— Bright, indirect

Water —— Drought tolerant

Humidity —— Normal

Airflow —— Normal to high

Temperature —— Normal to warm

Pet Friendly —— Yes

Native —— Mexico, Belize, Guatemala

THE HAPPY CAMPER

ALOE VERA

(*Aloe vera*)

BEST PAIRED WITH THESE PLANT PARENTS

The World Traveler
The Workin' 9 to 5
The Designer

SOIL RECIPE

First Date Mix
Desert Darling Mix

PROFILE

With its laid-back needs, tending to this healing plant is a joy for any plant parent. Indoor bright light mimics the perfect outdoor setting for aloe. The amount of light it gets will determine how quickly or slowly the soil dries up. Give it the time it needs to use up those resources and replenish consistently. The leaves will be plump and happy if the plant is well hydrated; if it gets too dry, it will send out a wrinkled SOS for some H_2O.

THRIVING CONDITIONS

Light —— Bright, indirect, or just indirect

Water —— Regular (drought tolerant during winter)

Humidity —— Normal

Airflow —— Normal

Temperature —— Normal to warm

Pet Friendly —— No

Native —— Africa and the Arabian Peninsula

THE PEACOCK

PINK LADY OR BIANCA INCH PLANT

(*Callisia repens* cv. Variegated)

**BEST PAIRED
WITH THESE
PLANT PARENTS**

The Workin' 9 to 5
The Designer
The Helicopter
The Collector

SOIL RECIPE

First Date Mix
Leaf Lover Mix

PROFILE

You will always take notice of this little show-off. With striking pink and green colors, the Pink Lady will instantly liven up any room with its vivid beauty. To help maintain that striking pink variegated foliage, place this beauty in a bright spot to carry on that bold color. It's perfect for the parent who would like to groom and pamper a plant, as this one requires more watering, pruning, and propagating to thrive.

THRIVING CONDITIONS

Light — Bright, indirect

Water — Regular

Humidity — Normal to high

Airflow — Normal

Temperature — Normal to warm

Pet Friendly — No

Native — Central and South
America and the
Caribbean

THE OVERACHIEVER

BURGUNDY RUBBER TREE

(*Ficus elastica* cv. Burgundy)

**BEST PAIRED
WITH THESE
PLANT PARENTS**

The World Traveler
The Workin' 9 to 5
The Designer
The Helicopter
The Collector

SOIL RECIPE

First Date Mix
Leaf Lover Mix
Huggable Mix

PROFILE

Don't pass up this luscious plant—it's a whole mood! While deceptive at first, the plant's thick leaves will surprise you when new growth emerges fire red and then deepens to a dark and dreamy burgundy as it unfurls and firms up. If you keep it happy and healthy, this prodigy will eventually grow from a houseplant to a statement tree.

THRIVING CONDITIONS

Light —— Bright or indirect

Water —— Regular

Humidity —— Normal to high

Airflow —— Normal to high

Temperature —— Normal to warm

Pet Friendly —— No

Native —— India and Malaysia

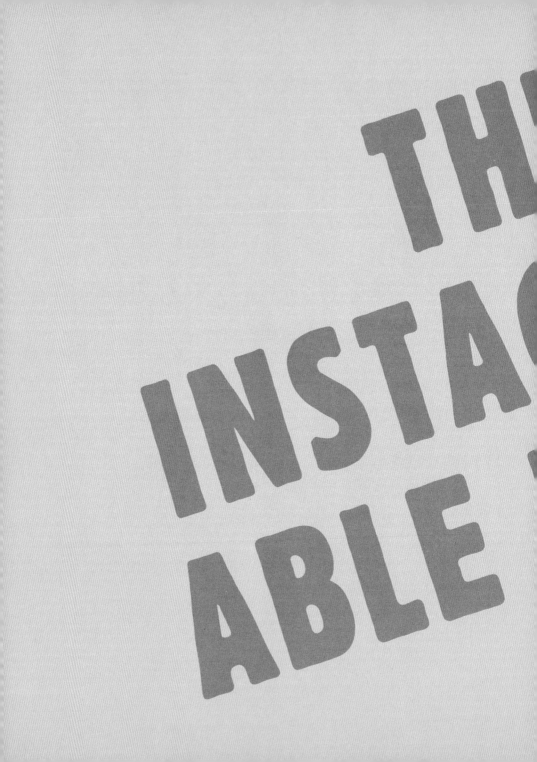

Y ou are scrolling through social media when you see it—plant eye candy—and you can't stop thinking about it. You've already imagined all the potential spots it could live in your space, and now all you need to do is find it. You scour the internet and local plant shops for the perfect one, but before you bring it home, you need to triple-check its care needs. Most of these photogenic babes require a bit more maintenance and attention than you might have assumed. If you're ready to dive in, though, they might just go viral for you.

As your plant-parent confidence rises, you'll find these plants are great to explore and take a chance on. Let's find out which ones you would double tap IRL.

THE MACRO INFLUENCER

THE MONSTERA
(*Monstera deliciosa*)

BEST PAIRED WITH THESE PLANT PARENTS

The Workin' 9 to 5
The Designer
The Helicopter
The Collector

SOIL RECIPE

Huggable Mix

PROFILE

When most people approach me about starting their plant journey, it's usually because they have been enraptured by this aspirational beauty. With leaves that scream "tropical paradise," the monstera has stolen the hearts of many a plant parent (including mine). It can elevate any room, but it does come at a price. Monsteras need ample space to unfurl their massive leaves and an environment that reminds them of the jungle from whence they came. I'm probably biased, but these lush leaves are way more than just Instagram hype.

THRIVING CONDITIONS

Light —— Indirect

Water —— Regular

Humidity —— Normal to high

Airflow —— Normal to high

Temperature —— Warm

Pet Friendly —— No

Native —— Central America and Australia

THE MICRO-INFLUENCER

THE GINNY OR "MINI" MONSTERA
(Rhaphidophora tetrasperma)

**BEST PAIRED
WITH THESE
PLANT PARENTS**

The Workin' 9 to 5
The Designer
The Helicopter
The Collector

SOIL RECIPE

First Date Mix
Leaf Lover Mix
Huggable Mix

PROFILE

The mini monstera may have gained clout from the monstera, but it quickly proved to many why it stands on its own as the perfectly sized version of the trendy plant. This plant first showed up on everyone's feed because it looked like a miniature version of the monstera. Plant parents learned quickly how rewarding this fast grower is and how stylish it can make a home. If you can get your hands on this plant, it will thrive in your space and may even take over your walls with its small but mighty leaves.

THRIVING CONDITIONS

Light —— Indirect or low

Water —— Regular

Humidity —— Normal to high

Airflow —— Normal to high

Temperature —— Warm

Pet Friendly —— No

Native —— Thailand and Malaysia

THE SOCIAL BUTTERFLY

BRASIL PHILODENDRON

(*Philodendron hederaceum* var. oxycardium "Brasil")

BEST PAIRED WITH THESE PLANT PARENTS

The World Traveler
The Workin' 9 to 5
The Designer
The Helicopter
The Collector

SOIL RECIPE

First Date Mix
Leaf Lover Mix
Huggable Mix
Desert Darling Mix
Sweetheart Mix

PROFILE

Everyone knows that one person who is always quick to make friends. The philodendron is popular in the plant world. Ranging in shape, size, texture, and care level, philodendrons are a match for any plant-parent personality and skill level. (Some velvet leaf philodendrons tend to be a little more difficult to come by.) The philodendrons adapt quickly to their environment and enjoy a more tropical atmosphere. Provide this baby with something to connect to and climb or a place from which to waterfall off a shelf, and it will never stop growing.

THRIVING CONDITIONS

Light —— Bright or indirect

Water —— Regular

Humidity —— Normal to high

Airflow —— Normal to high

Temperature —— Normal to warm

Pet Friendly —— No

Native —— Central America and the Caribbean

THE ECO-INFLUENCER

CACTI

**BEST PAIRED
WITH THESE
PLANT PARENTS**

The World Traveler
The Workin' 9 to 5
The Designer
The Collector

SOIL RECIPE

Desert Darling Mix

PROFILE

Cacti are smart about conserving their resources and adapting to their native harsh environments. Having balance and understanding the nature of this plant will prove vital for success. The cacti store water in their stems and therefore can happily tolerate long periods of drought. Knowing when they most need water and providing them with bright and warm conditions are keys to winning them over. But don't judge them by their spiny or spiky exteriors; they're really just watery softies on the inside.

THRIVING CONDITIONS

Light —— Bright

Water —— Regular (drought
               tolerant during winter)

Humidity —— Low to normal

Airflow —— Low to normal

Temperature —— Warm to hot

Pet Friendly —— No

Native —— North America,
               Colombia, Mexico,
               Chile, and Argentina

THE TRENDSETTER

CHINESE MONEY PLANT
or UFO Plant
(*Pilea peperomioides*)

**BEST PAIRED
WITH THESE
PLANT PARENTS**

The Workin' 9 to 5
The Designer
The Helicopter
The Collector

SOIL RECIPE

First Date Mix
Leaf Lover Mix

PROFILE

When the Chinese money plant started showing up on trendy Pinterest posts, this easy-to-multiply plant reached a level of fame never before seen in the plant community and became one of the most sought-after plants in the United States. It even reached trending social media heights with its own #friendshipplant hashtag. Like every good friendship, the pilea takes work and time to flourish. Its care needs might make it a bit challenging for some, but if you have a good, steady care routine for it, this plant will reward you endlessly. How can you say no to a plant this cute?

THRIVING CONDITIONS

Light —— Bright or indirect

Water —— Regular

Humidity —— Normal to high

Airflow —— Normal

Temperature —— Normal to warm

Pet Friendly —— Yes

Native —— China

THE BLOGGER

HOYA KRIMSON PRINCESS

(*Hoya carnosa* var. *variegata*)

BEST PAIRED WITH THESE PLANT PARENTS

The Workin' 9 to 5
The Helicopter
The Collector

SOIL RECIPE

First Date Mix
Huggable Mix
Desert Darling Mix

PROFILE

Coming in all different shapes, colors, sizes, and textures, the waxy-leafed hoya has been a popular houseplant since before the dawn of social media. The Krimson Princess is a perfect example of the beautiful pink-leafed options that hoyas come in. Like most photo-loving bloggers, lighting is essential, so make sure you provide your hoya with bright, indirect light for optimal growth. Side note: It's a slow grower until you find that sweet spot. With enough impressions, this plant might just reward you with the sweetest fuzzy blooms that will steal your heart and those of your followers.

THRIVING CONDITIONS

Light — Bright or indirect

Water — Regular

Humidity — Normal to high

Airflow — Normal to high

Temperature — Normal to warm

Pet Friendly — Yes

Native — Southern Asia, Southeast Asia, Polynesia, and Australia

THE ARTISTS

SUCCULENTS

**BEST PAIRED
WITH THESE
PLANT PARENTS**

The World Traveler
The Workin' 9 to 5

SOIL RECIPE

First Date Mix
Desert Darling Mix

PROFILE

Among the many kinds of succulents available, you'll find a huge range of alluring colors—pot them together to create a masterpiece! You may think that succulents are indestructible, but that's actually not the case. Succulents are sensitive to moisture and light and need a good bit of attention. Give a succulent too little light and it could stretch or grow, known as etiolation. Too much moisture in the air or soil, and it might rot; too little water, and your succulent will shrivel up and might even die. Like mixing the right paint color for the particular image, growing succulents is an art form.

THRIVING CONDITIONS

Light — Bright or indirect

Water — Regular (drought tolerant during winter)

Humidity — Low to normal

Airflow — Low to normal

Temperature — Normal to warm

Pet Friendly — No (though some varieties may be)

Native — Africa, North and South America, Europe

THE ICON

BIRD OF PARADISE
(Strelitzia nicolai)

BEST PAIRED WITH THESE PLANT PARENTS

The Designer
The Helicopter

SOIL RECIPE

First Date Mix
Leaf Lover Mix
Sweetheart Mix

PROFILE

Gracing the landscape of many a botanical garden, the coveted bird of paradise is an expert at making a statement. If you ever get to enjoy the rare experience of having one bloom for you indoors, you might feel overwhelmed by its striking birdlike flower. With the ability to grow several feet tall, the bird of paradise earns its name by transporting you to an island utopia. The large oval leaves will take up a lot of space, and they require a lot of humidity, but they are worth the effort.

THRIVING CONDITIONS

Light — Bright or indirect

Water — Regular

Humidity — High

Airflow — Low to normal

Temperature — Warm

Pet Friendly — No

Native — Southern Africa

THE BEAUTY VLOGGER

MAJESTY PALM
(*Ravenea rivularis*)

BEST PAIRED WITH THESE PLANT PARENTS

The Workin' 9 to 5
The Designer
The Collector

SOIL RECIPE

First Date Mix
Leaf Lover Mix
Sweetheart Mix

PROFILE

Bringing palms indoors can transform your space from ho-hum to shabby chic. Whether your style is bohemian, modern, or eclectic, the majesty palm knows how to contour any room flawlessly. Like most indoor palms, temperature control, light, and a watering routine are essential to please this beauty queen. It loves a dewy complexion, so be sure to water it consistently and pot it in a moisture-retaining soil.

THRIVING CONDITIONS

Light —— Bright or indirect

Water —— Regular

Humidity —— Normal to high

Airflow —— Normal to high

Temperature —— Warm to hot

Pet Friendly —— Yes

Native —— Madagascar

LEFT, LEFT, RIGHT, RIGHT, LEFT, RIGHT, SQUARE, CIRCLE, TRIANGLE, R1, R2, RIGHT, LEFT, RIGHT, X . . .

hile video games have plenty of cheats to help you along on your journey, there isn't an easy cheat for keeping plants in tip-top shape. People ask me for my secrets, but there really isn't a one-size-fits-all answer. Some "easy" plants can be hard for some plant parents, and some "hard" plants can be easy for others. It all comes down to the environment you're offering and the type of plant parent you are (or want to be). On top of that, some of these rare beauties aren't easily available and may require a bit of searching to find.

Whether you decided to start with the hard ones or you've leveled up gradually, these plants may put up a fight, but they're worth it for that bonus-level plant success.

THE MONARCH

CHINESE EVERGREEN LEGACY PINK

(*Aglaonema* cv. Legacy)

BEST PAIRED WITH THESE PLANT PARENTS

The Workin' 9 to 5
The Designer
The Helicopter
The Collector

SOIL RECIPE

First Date Mix
Leaf Lover Mix

PROFILE

Aglaonemas are cultivated in an array of colors and patterns, and they can be the crown jewel in your collection. Given the right balance of light and environment (humidity, temperature, and space), this regal plant can grow to be large and reign for decades. I've seen some aglaonemas that have been around since the 1970s! Your lighter-colored aglaonema will thrive in bright but indirect light, whereas the greener aglaonemas can tolerate more indirect light. Balancing the light and keeping the soil moist, the temperature warm, and the humidity high will help this plant leave a lasting legacy.

THRIVING CONDITIONS

Light — Low or indirect to bright

Water — Regular

Humidity — Normal to high

Airflow — Normal

Temperature — Normal to warm

Pet Friendly — No

Native — Asia and New Guinea

THE ARCHER

GREEN VELVET ALOCASIA
(OR ELEPHANT EAR), ALOCASIA FRYDEK

(*Alocasia micholitziana* cv. Frydek)

**BEST PAIRED
WITH THESE
PLANT PARENTS**

The Helicopter
The Collector

SOIL RECIPE

First Date Mix
Leaf Lover Mix
Sweetheart Mix

PROFILE

The striking alocasia can throw even the most experienced plant parents off their game. With a variety of challenges, like its propensity for attracting pests and its finicky environmental needs, this moving target can be difficult to hit. But when you finally pierce that humidity bull's-eye, the alocasia can be one of the most rewarding plants in your collection. Some variations are a little more forgiving (like the *Alocasia amazonica*), but even with the best care, an alocasia usually only holds three or four leaves until maturity (then it holds five or six).

THRIVING CONDITIONS

Light — Indirect

Water — Regular

Humidity — High

Airflow — Normal to high

Temperature — Normal to warm

Pet Friendly — No

Native — Asia and eastern
Australia

THE MELEE

ANTHURIUM CLARINERVIUM
(*Anthurium clarinervium*)

BEST PAIRED WITH THESE PLANT PARENTS

The Helicopter
The Collector

SOIL RECIPE

First Date Mix
Leaf Lover Mix
Huggable Mix
Desert Darling Mix
Sweetheart Mix

PROFILE

Testing your battle stamina, the anthurium calls for hand-to-hand combat since that seems to be the solution when keeping these plants indoors. This is the plant in my personal collection that I fight with the most. Even though I've lost strong anthuriums to my own mistakes, like thinking their leafy armor means they're hardier than they actually are, getting a handle on their many needs has made me a skilled plant warrior. These greenhouse-loving plants are humidity dependent. I've had to place most of my anthuriums in my caches, domes, and healing boxes just to keep them thriving, but it's all worth it for these thick-leaved, prehistoric-looking beauties.

THRIVING CONDITIONS

Light —— Bright indirect or indirect

Water —— Regular

Humidity —— High

Airflow —— Normal to high

Temperature —— Warm to hot

Pet Friendly —— No

Native —— Mexico, Colombia, and Ecuador

THE BARD

POLKA DOT BEGONIA

(*Begonia maculata*)

BEST PAIRED WITH THESE PLANT PARENTS

The Workin' 9 to 5
The Designer
The Helicopter
The Collector

SOIL RECIPE

First Date Mix
Leaf Lover Mix

PROFILE

The begonia has proven to be a crowd favorite, with its pleasing patterns and luscious coloring. Popular begonias, like the Polka Dot, are famous for their metallic silver spots and lush, red undersides, which also makes them suitable for lower light situations. Too much light, and you can run into a very crispy situation. When your begonia starts to sing for you, be sure to have all the instruments you need to tame that fast grower! For plant parents who enjoy being a little more hands-on, the begonia is always looking for a prune and is great for propagation.

THRIVING CONDITIONS

Light — Low or indirect

Water — Regular

Humidity — Medium to high

Airflow — Normal

Temperature — Normal to warm

Pet Friendly — No

Native — Africa, Central and South America, and Asia

THE MAGE

STAGHORN OR ELKHORN FERNS
(*Platycerium* spp.)

BEST PAIRED WITH THESE PLANT PARENTS

The Workin' 9 to 5
The Helicopter

SOIL RECIPE

First Date Mix
Leaf Lover Mix
Sweetheart Mix

PROFILE

It might take a little magic to keep a delicate fern living in your space. Some ferns, like the bird's nest, are a little more forgiving, whereas the staghorn fern, named for the beautiful antlerlike leaf shape that develops as it matures, might require an arsenal of plant powers. A great way to display this fern (or any) is to mount it and hang it. Mix the right amount of light, moisture, and humidity, and you'll command the almighty fern.

GREEN RULE OF THUMB

WATER MOUNTED PLANTS BY SOAKING IN A BUCKET FOR 10 MINUTES OR SHOWERING IT AND LETTING THE WATER RUN THROUGH.

THRIVING CONDITIONS

Light — Indirect or low

Water — Regular

Humidity — High

Airflow — Normal to high

Temperature — Warm

Pet Friendly — Yes

Native — Africa, Asia, and South America

THE WISE

RATTLESNAKE CALATHEA

(Calathea lancifolia)

**BEST PAIRED
WITH THESE
PLANT PARENTS**

The Workin' 9 to 5
The Designer
The Helicopter
The Collector

SOIL RECIPE

Desert Darling Mix

PROFILE

These gorgeously patterned plants grow along forest floors and are experts at adapting to their environment and conserving energy. Calatheas, commonly known as prayer plants, raise or roll up their leaves during the night, then spread them wide open during the day to capture the light. In the home, you can imitate the forest-floor preferences with humidity and moist soil. These wise plants conserve the light using their dark leafy undersides to constrict the light from passing through, thereby providing their lower light conditions.

THRIVING CONDITIONS

Light —— Bright, indirect to low

Water —— Regular

Humidity —— Medium to high

Airflow —— Normal

Temperature —— Warm

Pet Friendly —— Yes

Native —— North, Central, and South America

THE DRAGON

FIDDLE-LEAF FIG

(*Ficus lyrata*)

**BEST PAIRED
WITH THESE
PLANT PARENTS**

The Designer
The Helicopter

SOIL RECIPE

First Date Mix
Leaf Lover Mix

PROFILE

You've seen this gorgeous beast stretching across all the most amazing spaces, from the center of a room to a small corner. The fiddle-leaf fig knows how to leave a long-lasting impression. These native African plants are accustomed to bright light and high heat, with just a touch of humidity and an airtight watering schedule. Once your plant settles into its spot, it seems like there is no moving it around unless you want it to breathe fire, perish overnight, and become a myth that only a bard will sing about. Tame it well, and it just might reward you with a high score. Caution: A happy fiddle-leaf will grow large and treelike!

THRIVING CONDITIONS

Light — Bright

Water — Regular

Humidity — Normal to high

Airflow — Normal to high

Temperature — Warm

Pet Friendly — No

Native — West Africa

WHAT IS THE PLANT COMMUNITY?

Thanks to social media, plant lovers from around the world have found one another to spread love and support for plants and their parents. Whether they are sharing their care tips, searching for new plants, or just starting out on their journeys, there is room for everyone.

Start where you're most comfortable. There are lots of social platforms where the plant community is growing and thriving. Making real friends through Instagram was the very last thing I anticipated, but it happened so organically. Most IRL friendships form when you live in the same area and either decide to get a group of people together to go plant-shop hopping or just meet up at an event like a plant swap and agree on making a plant trade.

I suggest connecting with other plant parents on the platform where you feel comfortable. Whether your community is Instagram, like mine is, or an online forum, like Facebook, Twitter, or TikTok, it feels like there is a slice of plant community in every corner of the internet.

Not only will you find unexpected or much-needed advice, but you'll also be able to connect with your neighborhood plant community so that you can set up swaps and get-togethers. Some of my favorite plants are the ones I've received from friends because they are associated with that person and that day, and it always brings a smile to my face when I look at those particular plants. This natural bond happens, and it's such a joyous feeling.

When I created *Apartment Botanist*, I remember being nervous that people inside and outside the plant community would look down on how passionate I was and that I expressed how plants made me feel. Almost immediately, however, I was embraced by the community. This relationship propagated endless help, encouragement, and positivity. I could never have anticipated the amount of kindness I would receive. Remember, communities thrive with a mutual give-and-take. But most importantly, always remember to be kind and respectful—and your true, plant-loving self!

Shopping for plants doesn't have to be a solo journey! I love gathering a small group of friends, plant lovers or not, and going together around to the local plant shops. It's a great way to support small local businesses, and it's also a way to gauge plant prices. It's a wonderful, joyous way to explore new shops and form close relationships with fellow plant parents.

If there aren't events happening locally, I highly encourage you to create your own. Form friendships with your local plant merchants and see if they would be willing to host a plant event or a plant swap to bring together people in the local community. If you can't— or have a hard time connecting in real life—there are amazing groups on Instagram and Facebook you can always be a part of. Don't be afraid to reach out or to make the first move to connect with other plant parents, no matter how you do it.

BUYING PLANTS ONLINE

B ack when I was beginning to explore the world of rare plants, the whole concept of buying a plant online and having it shipped to me in a box was totally baffling. Was it safe for the plant? Was I going to get duped? Will the plant be dead when I open the box?

While most major cities are home to some amazing plant shops, I learned quickly that if I wanted variety, I needed to get over my fears and hesitations. I had built a wish list of plants I wanted, so I did what I normally do in moments of curiosity: I started researching what plants could be shipped and who had the expertise to do it.

I put in a pretty large order for the middle of winter, and it turned out okay. It wasn't as scary as I had imagined, but some of my fears were confirmed and a number of the plants I ordered ended up needing a good amount of TLC.

Here's what I'll say after years of perfecting the art of online plant shopping: It's normal to lose a leaf or for a plant to look depleted and stressed, but if that makes you nervous, then buying online may not be the right thing for you—at least not right now. If you're ready to take the plunge, though, the following are guidelines that have proven the most successful for me:

1. **Buy plants from reputable people and businesses.**
   Try to look for sellers that have amassed a large clientele and have been selling for years. If they have lots of repeat customers and are recommended often by other plant parents, it's probably a great shop to start with. Don't be afraid to ask people how their experiences were, both good and bad. Proceed with caution when it comes to individual sellers, especially those on Facebook and eBay! Even though you can get a bargain or come up with a trade with others, if you do meet up with people in real life, always be sure it's in a public setting.

2. **Check reviews.**
   Look for sellers with lots of reviews that look genuine and descriptive. This paints a great picture of what your potential experience may be. There have been so many times I ignored bad reviews, and I quickly learned my lesson.

3. **Check the seller's or shop's policies.**

   Never be afraid to ask about return policies or damaged/lost plant procedures if they're not stated anywhere. Know and understand how these shops run their businesses.

4. **Photos.**

   If you are shopping small, ask for photos, especially if it's from an individual seller. Photos can ensure you get what you are paying for and preferably provide you with an accurate idea of the size and health of the plant.

5. **Avoid preorders.**

   I can't recall a time when a friend or I had a plant preorder go well. If the plants are not ready to sell, don't purchase them. A lot of sellers will offer preorders, meaning there is no guarantee they will become anything more than imaginary.

6. **If a price or deal seems too good to be true, it probably is.**

   Research the plants you're looking to buy and shop around before you hit the purchase button. Go with your gut and don't be afraid to ask the community for its opinions. Plant prices are constantly rising as demand grows, but it's still great to have a baseline.

7. **Clarify with the seller what you will be receiving.**

   Is it a cutting (no roots but viable nodes), a rooted cutting (a cutting with formed roots, typically water propagated), a fully rooted plant (a plant potted in soil with an established root system), a plant shipped "bare root," or a fully rooted and potted plant? This will help you better prepare for the plant's arrival. If you are purchasing a cutting, keep in mind that it will be up to you to establish that cutting's root system.

8. **Wait for warm weather to purchase plants.**
    Ask or find sellers who will wait for good weather to ship their plants. You don't want to ship plants during extreme heat or extreme cold because you can't count on the trucks or facilities to be temperature controlled.

9. **If you are purchasing internationally, be sure that the sellers provide a phytosanitary certificate.**
    This certificate provides documentation for the plant and declares that it has gone through a cleaning process. Plants that are shipped internationally are shipped bare root (i.e., no soil, no pot). Keep in mind that it's a lot riskier for the plant to be shipped that way, and it will probably take a lot more effort to acclimatize it once it arrives. Make sure the reward is worth the risk!

10. **After your plant arrives safe and sound in its new home, give it time to adjust to its new environment.**
    Don't place it in bright light right out of the box. Beyond isolating and repotting to prevent an infestation (see page 57), the plant will need some time to recuperate. It's better to anticipate some damage than to demand perfection. A plant is being shipped in a box. That's a lot of stress on a plant, so it might lose some leaves and may need some TLC to recoup. If you ordered from an outdoor nursery, it's more likely to have pests, which is normal. Take the extra step to clean the plant and use preventative measures.

11. **Set a budget for your purchases.**
    Don't let the pressure of trendy or expensive plants drain you dry. Try looking for trades or other ways you can obtain new plants that won't break the bank. This is another reason why

cultivating your plant community is helpful! If you're patient enough and do your research, you're patient enough to wait for a good price—even on a dream plant.

12. **Avoid seeds.**
    Buying houseplant seeds online is almost always a scam. You have no way of knowing what you are actually purchasing.

13. **Always use PayPal.**
    Even if it feels more convenient to pay via a third party, like Facebook, always pay directly through PayPal. Be mindful of how long you have to file a dispute or claim.

GREEN RULE OF THUMB

SET YOURSELF SOME TYPE OF GUIDELINE OR BUDGET. PLANTS ARE THERE TO MAKE YOU HAPPY, NOT STRESS YOU OUT FINANCIALLY. I ALWAYS SAY THAT IF YOU'RE PATIENT ENOUGH AND DO YOUR RESEARCH, YOU CAN FIND YOUR DREAM PLANT FOR THE RIGHT PRICE—EVEN IF IT TAKES A LITTLE MORE TIME.

HOW TO NOT FALL FOR A PLANT SCAM

A couple of things may be running through your head when you hear the phrase "plant scam." One: How is that even a thing? Two: Who would fall for something so silly? Well, it's definitely a thing, and I've fallen for a couple!

The worst plant scam I ever experienced was on a private Facebook group. The villain of this story—let's call him CC—knew just how to rip off the plant folks. I was in search of a plant on my ever-growing wish list when I stumbled across his group. So many things checked out: He communicated well, especially when someone was interested in making a purchase; he came highly recommended; and he had shipped plants before.

During this go-around, he promised hundreds of people plants coming from Thailand. He took what must have been thousands of dollars in preorder sales (which I now know is a big red flag), and he told everyone he had a contact in Thailand with a nursery and was getting a great deal on a lot of rare and normally expensive plants. He posted photos, provided updates, and would offer more plants if people wanted to add to their preorders.

Weeks after the initial order, people in the group started inquiring about their plants and when they were going to be shipped. The promised dates to ship had come and gone, and CC never followed up.

While most people were able to get their money back through PayPal, hundreds of people paid him via different means and couldn't get a refund. Thankfully, I got the majority of my money back, but I did add a $20 plant to my order that he encouraged me to purchase through Facebook, which I now know is a big no-no because they do not refund your money. I had learned a very important $20 life lesson. Thanks, CC!

All in all, ask questions! If sellers are genuine and true, they won't and shouldn't have any issues with buyers asking reasonable questions about their products. If they do give you a hard time, move along; they won't be the first or the last seller to offer that plant you've been looking for.

And for whoever needs to hear this, *don't worry*. One day you'll get that plant on your wish list, so don't rush it. When you have an awful feeling about a seller, listen to your intuition and shop elsewhere.

✳ Avoid individual random sellers, most notably sellers without consistent stock. Proceed with caution when it comes to Facebook Marketplace and eBay!

✳ Avoid preorders. I know this is the millionth time I've said this, but I can't stress enough that preorders never seem to work out in a buyer's favor.

✳ Check people's social media. In my scenario, CC used a false identity and had no other social media I could find—big red flag!

✳ Always use PayPal. Pay through PayPal directly, and be mindful of how long you have to file a dispute or claim.

HOW TO MAKE A JUNGLE FIT IN YOUR HOME

t's no secret that my plants get prime real estate in my apartment since plants need ideal light, temperature, and humidity to survive and thrive. If you intend to collect more than a few plants, these ideal locations fill up quickly—especially if you're like me.

Since space is always a hot commodity, here are a few quick tricks to help you save every last bit of it:

WALLS ARE YOUR FRIEND: When every windowsill or sunny spot on the floor has been filled, it's time to start looking up! Shelves are the perfect way to make more room for plants. Choose a wall that receives a decent amount of light and get creative with your plant placement! I love using figurine display mini shelves— they are perfect for a tiny wall spot. Whatever you choose, keep in mind you don't want to block the plant from its light source.

MIRROR, MIRROR ON THE WALL: Aside from making your space look more expansive, having some mirrors around can benefit your plants, too. Try placing decorative mirrors in spots that can reflect the light onto the plants. I personally love using a recycled mirror behind and under a few of my plants so that when the light shines in on them, it bounces onto the backs and undersides of the leaves and distributes more light throughout the space.

DANGLE THOSE PLANTS FROM THE CEILING: Hanging planters are another way to create more space in your home. Maybe you can even make a hanging shelf to place multiple plants on it.

BE THRIFTY: I love going to thrift stores and flea markets to find unique items that I can use for my plants around the apartment. Things like domes and stands are always helpful, but it's also fun to think outside the pot. For example, I turned a thrifted 90-gallon fish tank into a plant hospital.

GROWING PAINS: Another reason you might run out of space is that your plant community is growing! Look at you! You could move your thriving plants, but if you'd rather leave them where they are, you can prune them back and even take cuttings for propagation, if that's your thing.

HOW TO TRAIN YOUR PLANTS: If you've got a plant that naturally grows on a tree, you can train your plant to climb the walls in different ways. For example, you can use Command hooks to give them a hand or moss poles (essentially a stick with tied sphagnum moss) to provide them with a vertical moment. Purchase something safe, like garden Velcro, and attach the stem along the moss pole. Keep the moss moist so that the plant's aerial roots attach to the pole. You could also look for a trellis or stick to help your plant climb up.

BE INSPIRED: Find what works for you. This is a perfect chance for you to turn to aspirational social media or look to the plant community for suggestions, tips, and DIY solutions. There are so many amazing plant parents around the world who curate amazing and unique spaces—there is always something to learn and discover.

PLANT CARE IS SELF-CARE

pening up is difficult, but plants will never judge you. Caring for my plants is a safe space for me. Through all my personal hardships, having plants to care for has helped me heal. In my opinion, there are a few key aspects of caring for plants that are actually caring for yourself:

QUIET TIME/MEDITATION: No matter where you live in the world, having a moment of silence and just being able to spend time with your plants is a calming and soothing experience. I love to have my coffee and walk around my plants, looking for new growth. Also, taking the time to meditate or sit with my daily intentions is a relaxing way to start my day alongside my plants.

WATERING AND SOUND: Even though this can be a lot of work, I love watering my plants. It's another bonding experience I have with them. I love seeing them perk up after a good shower! I also use this time to listen to music or a favorite podcast.

REPOTTING: Getting your hands dirty is fun. It feels like you're a kid again, playing in nature. Getting the soil in between your fingers and potting up a plant can be very therapeutic.

DESIGNING: Who else gets that giddy feeling when they bring home a new plant baby? I love finding the perfect spot in my home. Plants are excellent at making your space feel like your home.

SHOPPING: Even if you don't buy anything, going plant shopping can be such a refreshing experience, especially when you're surrounded by all that green. I also love that you can go plant shopping with your friends—you never know who you might turn into a new plant parent!

SHARING: A big part of why I love propagating plants is that I'm then able to share them with friends and family. There is something special about having that connection to others.

RESCUING: Being able to bring a plant back from ill health to its full potential is such a magical experience. It always takes patience, and it doesn't always work, but when it does, it is a most exciting and rewarding experience.

DOCUMENTING: I love photographing my plants. Having visual proof of your plant's growth is so satisfying and fun to watch. This is a great way to bond and keep a record of your collection.

BREAKFASTING: I love spending time with my plants when I first wake up. Eating a meal alongside one of my plant babies is such a nice, calm way to start off my day. It is a great chance to have an up-close look at the plant.

PLANT SPA DAY: Bringing my plants to the shower for a rainforest experience is something I do every so often. It's a perfect little mini spa day for the plants and some great time to simultaneously care for myself, too. I like to put a face mask on while I wait for the plants to dry off. It's a relaxing way to wind down the day.

For me, caring for plants has always been a privilege. I feel happy when I wake up and see my plants living in harmony with my family. I always say, " I *get* to care for my plants," never "I *have* to."

PLANTS MAKE THE WORLD GROW ROUND

Being a plant parent is not always easy, but I'm grateful. Through occasionally failing, I've learned to keep trying and not to feel shame about or doubt my abilities as a plant parent. I've strengthened my confidence in myself and learned how to shake off any feelings of self-consciousness. One of the biggest lessons that plants have taught me is that it's okay to start over. Sometimes plants don't work out, and experiencing this repeatedly with plants has given me the confidence to start fresh and do what's best for me with my plants and in life.

It's pretty amazing to think that plants teach me so many things that I can apply to my everyday life. I've learned a lot about patience, and I've also become more gentle with others and with myself. I've also learned that with patience, anything can grow.

There is no universal answer to plant care. All plants have little quirks, but part of the fun of being a plant parent is developing your skills and learning from your failures. Did I mention that it's 100 percent okay to fail? Because it is, and you will.

Like Charon, I've rowed quite a few plant souls across the river Styx into the afterlife. It's sad, but it happens to even the most seasoned plant parents.

Maybe for some, plants are just those cool accessories that decorate your home, but for me (and probably for you), plants—and caring for plants—are great acts of self-care and community building. *You* get to choose your plant family, and it doesn't need to be large, trendy, or expensive to make you happy.

Whether you are a plant parent with 1 plant or 500, know that everyone's journey with plants is unique. No matter how you get here, I'm sure happy you did.

GLOSSARY

In this book I've shared with you all the tips, red flags, and joys of plant buying, growing, gifting, and loving. By now, you can probably identify which plant thrives in low light or how to tackle a pest problem. But if you are still stuck on an idea or a word, don't stress. This glossary is for you to thumb through quickly so you can feel confident the next time you step into a plant shop.

ACCLIMATE: Getting a plant used to a new environment.

AERATED ROOT: Root that is aboveground and needs to be provided with a decent amount of airflow and moisture from the humidity in the air.

BARE ROOT: Method of shipping a plant whereby the roots of the plant are exposed and free of soil or any medium.

CACHE: A pot that has no drainage holes. Cache pots are made of various materials, such as ceramic, cement, terra-cotta, plastic, or fiberglass. Most plant parents will insert a nursing pot into a cache pot.

CUT LINE: During propagation, the line under the node where you make the cut.

DOME: A round glass enclosure for a plant to help increase its humidity.

ETIOLATION: When a plant is growing in partial or no light, and it stretches for the sun. Telltale signs of etiolation include long, weak stems, small leaf growth, and a pale yellow color, owing to a lack of chlorophyll.

GROW LIGHTS: This is a bulb or sometimes LED that helps plants grow. Perfect solution if you have little to no natural sunlight, as this artificial light source provides a light spectrum similar to the sun.

HEALING BOX: This is a term I coined for a clear plastic bin that helps delicate or regrowing plants heal by retaining humidity. I use this in conjunction with grow lights.

INFLORESCENCE: The cluster of flowers on a stem.

NODE: The knuckle on the stem of a plant where buds, new stems, or aerial roots grow.

PETIOLE: The stalk of a plant that connects a leaf to the stem and allows the leaf and the products of photosynthesis to be transported throughout the rest of the plant.

RHIZOME: The swollen root of a plant that grows just underground or at surface level, from which shoots and roots emerge.

SOIL LINE: The top surface of the soil, where the plant divides between top growth and root system.

TERRARIUM: An enclosed container (usually clear) that contains soil, potted plants, and water.

VARIEGATION: The lack of chlorophyll in a plant that makes it appear white, light green, or yellow. Most white sections of a plant will eventually brown and die off, as variegation often is a mutation.

VIVARIUM: An enclosure that houses both plant life and animals, typically built to imitate their natural environments.

ACKNOWLEDGMENTS

Plants Are My Favorite People brought me so much joy to create. I'm thankful for the many beautiful individuals who helped me get here and guided me through writing this book.

My Family

My mom, for believing in me back when I was selling beaded bracelets on a stoop in Brooklyn to now writing my very own book. You always knew I could accomplish anything I set my mind to, even if all the odds were against me. You always had my back, and I'm proud to be your daughter. Thank you for fostering my creativity and my humor, all things I get from you!

Daddy, thank you for going along with every out-of-the-box idea I've ever had; you always supported me through them. It makes my heart so full watching you enjoy and love your plants.

My sister, Giana, because of you, I grew up knowing endless kindness. Thank you for always being my safe place.

My Micah, I can't believe I get to have you in my life. You accept me full-heartedly and embrace every creative thought I've ever had. You always see my potential and have no reservations reminding me of it. Thank you for embarking on this *planty* adventure with me and being part of all that makes me smile.

Bobby, thank you for being supportive and proud of all my accomplishments. Thank you for giving plants a chance in your life.

To my niece, Abrielle, and nephew, Oliver, thank you for the belly laughs when I needed them the most. Your unconditional love is the joy and light of our family. I can't wait to teach you both all about plants.

My Friends

Angela Alba, your love and support are something I have cherished ever since the days of the Lion and the Tin Man. I'm so lucky to have your wisdom and guidance that are beyond your years. Thank you for encouraging me to start a plantstagram and for reminding me to do what I want and what I love to do.

Carly Elkin, I've been fortunate since day one when we began as roommates, and it quickly turned us into best friends. Thank you for always knowing how to make me laugh and never being afraid to be silly with me.

Ray Quartuci, my friend in heaven, I know you would be proud and cheering me on. I miss you every day.

My Team

Noah Ballard, I must have done something right in a past life to have you as my agent. Thank you for making me feel confident in this new process and always believing in the book and me.

Vivian Lee, thank you for your kindness and guidance from the moment I met you. You helped take this tiny seed and make it into a fully grown "plant" book.

The Clarkson Potter team, thank you for trusting in me and in the importance of plants and the parents that love them. Thank you to Gabrielle Van Tassel for giving me the encouragement, the opportunity, and the guidance throughout my first book.

A big thank you to Lucila Perini for capturing my imagination and breathing life into these plants and their personalities.

My Community

To the most remarkable community without whom none of this would be possible. Thank you for giving plants a place in your homes and, more importantly, in your hearts.

To the old, new, and future plant parents, I hope you take time for your passion for growing, don't hesitate to let your thoughts and ideas propagate, and, finally, let your intuition thrive.

INDEX